A Rope of Writers

Graham Wilson

A ROPE OF WRITERS

A look at mountaineering literature in Britain

Millrace

First published in Great Britain in 2006 by
Millrace
2a Leafield Road, Disley
Cheshire SK12 2JF
www.millracebooks.co.uk

ISBN: 1 902173 22 8 (to Dec 2006)
ISBN: 978 1 902173 22 1 (from Jan 2007)

Typeset in Berthold Baskerville.
Printed and bound in the United Kingdom
by MPG Books Ltd, Victoria Square, Bodmin, Cornwall.

Acknowledgements

My appreciation is due to all authors and publishers who have informed my reading on mountaineering in Britain, but particularly The Climbers' Club, The Fell & Rock Club and The Rucksack Club, not only for permission to quote from their journals and guides in this book, but also for providing a significant reservoir of climbing reminiscence and information for future readers to enjoy. In addition, I would like to single out the help, encouragement and advice that I have received from Dave Hewitt, Peter Hodgkiss, Jim Perrin and Ken Wilson in my search both for availability of material and permission to use it.

Every effort was made to contact the authors, original publishers and other relevant parties but this proved to be not always possible. I apologise for any apparent discourtesy and hope the publication of a book's details in the text and in the bibliography will suffice as a substitute. Specifically, my thanks are due to Anne Murray for the extract from *Undiscovered*

Scotland by W H Murray; The Ernest Press for the extracts from *Creagh Dhu Climber* by Jeff Connor, *Climbing in the British Isles* by W P Haskett Smith and *May The Fire Be Always Lit* by I D S Thomson; Bâton Wicks for the extracts from *The Ridiculous Mountains* by G J F Dutton, *Always a Little Further* by Alastair Borthwick and *The Black Cliff* by Jack Soper, Ken Wilson and Peter Crew; *The Herald* for an extract from an article by Jock Nimlin in *The Glasgow Herald* on April 22nd 1950; Victor Gollancz, a division of Orion Publishing Group, for the extract from *One Man's Mountains* by Tom Patey.

Graham Wilson
August 2006

Contents

Genesis

I suppose it depends on where you're brought up. The environment shapes the culture, which in turn shapes you. At the time, the town of Sunderland was balanced on a tripod of coalmining, shipbuilding and football. Life for most was entwined within this framework. Monday to Friday was work and Saturday was Roker Park, hoping the blessed Len would once more keep the overbearing southerners at bay. Sunday, for me, was a chance to go climbing–not, I may add, in the local environment. The mighty range of the Tunstall Hills, that quivers around the cusp of 300 feet above sea level, and the uncharted Claxheugh Rock, a crumbling sandstone rampart that sustained a bank of the River Wear, fell somewhat short of the stuff that dreams, or even modest ambitions, are made of. No handy gritstone edges for the north-east lads to lasso with their mother's clothes-line.

I say lads, for there were definitely two of us who

appeared from time to time, swaddled with rope, on the upper deck of the tram, to the understandable concern of our elders and sniggering references to Albert Pierrepoint from the less mature. In fact, this might not be strictly correct. Even Sunderland might have converted to petrol by this time but if trams were good enough for the Salford lads, a tram is good enough for me to add colour to the throw of a historical sweep. In any event, we duly discovered Crag Lough, a lump of quartz dolerite that Hadrian had incorporated in the Wall which signified the end of civilisation as he knew it.

A connection (a somewhat optimistic collective noun) of trains, followed by a walk-in which on some days seemed to assume Himalayan proportions, brought us not only to the crag but, as often as not, to the very fount of our escalatory knowledge. Arthur, for such was he, seemed to spend much of his time commuting between the foot of Hadrian's Buttress, under which he sat constructing thick woollen socks out of mammoth strands of Harris tweed, and the Twice Brewed Inn where he was happy to recall to those who would listen his former glories. We were happy to listen and supplement our meagre knowledge with his wisdom. Arthur said he had done all the climbs on the crag and, as any guidebook was out of print, he became our only point of reference. He was certainly very good at names and grades but a little less secure on detail, particularly the exact nature of moves that were more than ten feet off the ground. So, for the most part, he sat at the foot of his crag, safely out of range of any falling objects, offering us advice that veered between the encouraging and the sanguine, a latter-day combination of Prometheus, the Delphic Oracle and Madame Defarge.

Sad to say, Arthur's knowledge of *Where to Climb in the British Isles* was considerably less than that of Edward C Pyatt, whose book of that title was then in the throes of production. Arthur's remained fixed within the limits of this particular part of Northumberland. It seemed that we were similarly bound to the no man's land that lay between the dark satanic mills and the blue remembered hills, with no greater threat to our livers than the more virulent outpourings of Federation Ale. Then an odd thing happened. Skulking, as was my wont, around the stacks of the local library, I chanced upon a shelf labelled Pastimes and Other Entertainments. There, between *Lunchtime Treats for the Thrifty Housewife* and *Needlework for Novices*, was a recent acquisition, *Mountaineering in Britain,* by the said Pyatt in conjunction with a Ronald W Clark. Unable to believe my luck, I swiftly registered my temporary ownership.

The contents were a revelation. It was clear that Britain abounded with cliffs that would put Crag Lough in the shade and our summer holiday in the Lake District immediately took on a new dimension. At the due date, I returned the book reluctantly to its proper protective custody but at once regretted that I had not taken greater note, quickly realising there were a number of areas that could have borne closer examination. I also assumed that a work of this breadth and interest would be in constant demand. To my surprise, there were no takers over the next few months, with the only stamped dates on the fly-leaf reflecting my own enthusiasm. Perhaps, after all, we were the only two lads in Sunderland who had found, if not an alternative, at least an addition to football.

Of all the areas of interest, it was the bibliography that most excited. Nearly 150 volumes were listed, each promising to flesh out the bones of the Clark/Pyatt history. I persuaded the Librarian to scour her branch offices for anything remotely containing an appropriate reference—*Climbing Roses and Other Ramblers* was, I recall, thrown up in the general enthusiasm—but the supply was generally scarce. Guidebooks, the ultimate quest, were particularly conspicuous by their absence and many an hour was spent in transcribing in longhand the convoluted meanderings of the heirs of Smith and Jones, rather than in appreciation of Salmon's *Jurisprudence* or Underhill on *Tort*.

When I was unable to beg or borrow, I was forced to buy and no second-hand bookshop was passed without toothcomb inspection. My only criteria were novelty and price, as it was content rather than appearance that was the overriding consideration. My status as bibliophile was ultimately exposed when I visited an upmarket antiquarian bookseller in one of the more fashionable parts of London. In response to my usual expansive request to be shown anything 'Mountaineering', I was presented from a locked, glass-fronted case with a selection varying from collected Victorian woodcuts to, *inter alia*, the leather-bound, privately-printed memoirs of Gentlemen in the Caucasus. Though some were of interest, all exceeded the budget and I started to demur. There was a pause, punctuated with a sharp intake of breath, before an assistant was summoned and instructed to 'Take the gentleman down to the basement. It appears he is after a reading copy.'

Over the years, the library grew sporadically. When retirement beckoned, I bought a copy of Sheppard's *Book Dealers in the British Isles*, with a plan to work through the listings in a relatively systematic manner. This evolved into a series of multi-purpose excursions which combined a variety of pleasures. A typical example might be: train to Church Stretton, a visit to Church Stretton Books, a walk round the Malverns, concluding with a sample of the local brew. The grand design faltered on a failing hip but that is another story, as is the dismay of my bank manager as my financial situation returned to the black.

But in this brief encounter I discovered two things. First, that I had arrived too late. The days when you might find a first edition of *Rock Climbing in the English Lake District* by O G Jones sandwiched on a shelf between *The Best Way to Breed Ferrets* and *Fly-fishing on the Tyne* were long gone. Second, the specialist dealer had cornered the market and also controlled the price. There seemed no alternative but to pay the going rate (bank manager's interest resurrected) but, as with all pendulums, there was a return swing. The availability of cyberspace meant that there were search engines at the collector's disposal which made previous combs more coarse curry than fine tooth. Moreover, particular publishers seemed willing to provide their own reprints of long-deceased old favourites, Haskett Smith's *Climbing in the British Isles* by the Ernest Press and a combined volume of the Murray classics *Mountaineering in Scotland* and *Undiscovered Scotland* by Diadem Books being cases in point. In addition, the centenary celebrations of the older climbing clubs prompted them to produce anthologies of the better articles that had appeared in their journals.

The discovery of Neate had, on me, a profound effect. *Mountaineering and its Literature* was first published in 1978 and listed books pertaining to mountaineering which had been written, for the most part, from a British perspective. A revised and enlarged edition appeared in 1986. My own novitiate book-collecting activities had suffered a similar insularity to my early climbing experience and the appearance of such terms as 'Neate starred' in the dealers' catalogues caused more confusion than enlightenment.

Eventually all became clear when I acquired a copy of the first edition. As a result, the previous scatter-gun approach began to develop a more particular aim: the collection of books that dealt primarily with mountaineering in the British Isles.

Neate's premature death left a void and clearly there is a need for an update. New writers have appeared and the established have extended their repertoire. Additionally, sympathetic publishers like Bâton Wicks, the Ernest Press and Millrace have offered an opportunity otherwise denied in the present publishing climate. I mention an update, but hasten to add that the pages that follow have no pre-tension to fill that role. They shine a light on a few rather than illuminate the many and the approach is generic rather than chronological or comprehen-sive. In fact, the ground covered goes little further than the later Neate.

There are three reasons for this, all of which may smack of making a virtue out of necessity. The first is that the chosen watershed coincides with the bulk of my own reading and the limits of my climbing ambition. I felt that if I investigated a spread from Haskett Smith's *Climbing in the British Isles* to Soper, Wilson and Crew's *The Black Cliff,* I had a reasonable chance of knowing what I was writing about. The second reason is that, from a certain perspective, mountaineering in Britain, as opposed to British mountaineering, had reached some sort of closure by the 1970s. The great challenges of England and Wales had been met, Scotland had been opened up and the likes of the winter traverse of the Cuillin Ridge had been completed. Climbers tended to drift away from the mountains to the warmer and drier climes of the coast. Relative affluence and ease of travel suggested Mediterranean limestone or the grandeur of Yosemite, rather than slimy rocks and frozen fingers. And the final reason is that most of what has been written in the last twenty-five years is retrospective and remains rooted in the climbing tradition threaded through Jones, Kirkus and Brown. Of course, there are new lines, and even new cliffs, but these seem more a branch than a further growth of the trunk. Today you are more likely to find the local aspirant trampolining off a crash-mat in Water-cum-Jolly than struggling unprotected on the crux of Right Unconquerable.

At the very least, I felt that a particular tradition had come to an end. A tradition that began when a man reported back that he had left his handkerchief tied to the top of an apparently inaccessible obelisk on Great Gable and concluded with the announcement (albeit in rather flatter vowels), 'Well, that's that bugger sorted!' at the top of a misted cliff on Snowdon. The book's title attempts to reflect this continuity. Just as a succession of climbers has led through in the solution of ever harder problems, so does literature use its own combined tactics. In the mirror of reading you often catch a glimpse of what and how you think or feel. Such moments can encourage a further generation to polish its own reflections and add them to the common store.

In the Beginning

There was the Golden Age. And in the Golden Age of mountaineering the most noted of its early writings was contained in a collection entitled *Peaks, Passes and Glaciers*, compiled by John Ball, the first President of the Alpine Club. Such was the book's success that the Club thought it best to report the doings of its membership and other kindred spirits in a regularly produced journal which would further cover 'everything useful to mountaineers'. By definition, the mountains described were the Alps or, occasionally, the greater ranges beyond. There was neither need nor call for such a detailed examination of the hills of Britain. An exceptional feat, such as Haskett Smith's ascent of Napes Needle or a winter ascent of some great Scottish Gully, might have appeared in some annexe or other, couched in the appropriately apologetic tone.

Nor was there any need for an instructional manual. Alpinists were a close-knit group where the experienced tutored the novice. Coming from similar well-heeled backgrounds (the hire of a guide for the Matterhorn would in today's terms have cost around £400 and you might need two), the Old Boy network would have been finely tuned to give all the support and advice necessary. You were invited to join a party at Wasdale or Zermatt and the rest took care of itself.

As the nineteenth century came to an end, things changed and the close-knit group felt threatened. The growth of public transport meant that the hills became more easily available to a large proportion of the population and the 'tourists' soon found their way to the likes of Snowdon and Scafell Pike. But it was, perhaps, the effect of another technological advance that had the more significant implication for the future of mountain climbing. The development of the camera meant that for the first time the rock-climbing mountaineer could be seen in action, balancing with apparent nonchalance on scarcely visible holds over a variety of alarming voids. These images seemed to provoke public interest (O G Jones was reputedly drawn to the sport after seeing a photograph of the Needle in a popular magazine) and official indignation in equal measure. Yet, despite the foreboding of coroners and certain sections of the Press, visiting and climbing the hills of Britain became a popular activity.

These newcomers had no in-built coterie to guide them and, inevitably, some of the parvenus came to grief. As this was the age of self-help, it is not surprising that books sprang up to instruct the tyro and warn the unwary. One of the first of these was *British Mountaineering* by Claude E Benson, published in 1909. The author was an established member of the climbing community and an enthusiastic hunter of foxes in the Lake District. Secure in these weighty qualifications, he set out to impart his knowledge and opinion, not only to the beginner but also to the native rock climber who might have the presumption to assume that success in this sphere qualified him as a full-blown Alpine mountaineer.

If the reader, as is often the case, were to skip the introductory chapter and start at what appears the meat of the matter, he would quickly realise that Benson had chosen his title with some care. This is not a book that just tells you where to climb in Britain but rather how to make the most of the climbing that the country offers. The novice, after being properly equipped and initiated in the various mysteries such as the alternative methods of removing the kinks from a wet hemp rope or why, in an emergency, brandy is preferable to whisky, is then sent on a graduated course that passes through the varying stages of Rambling, Scrambling and, finally, Rock Climbing.

Even if the tone is somewhat didactic, it is all good sensible advice, born of long experience. By 'Rambling', Benson means fellwalking rather than pottering around country lanes and it is the hills of the Lake District that act as his model. He first takes the reader to the map, in this case of the fell of Grassmoor and its satellites, and conducts an imaginary expedition, pointing out where to go and what to avoid. The reader can then repeat the experience on the ground in relative safety and, with later reference to the model, increase or modify his own understanding of what is involved. The potential dangers are not ignored but nor are they overstated. The author does not condemn *walking* alone and positively encourages a certain degree of boldness based on his own experience.

In my early days I was a great deal troubled with headiness on ridges, until it occurred to me to estimate not the ease, but the difficulty of falling off, and to my surprise I found that it would require a distinct and definite effort on my part to do so.

Any of the previous instructional manuals had tended to jump directly from Mountain Walking to Climbing on either Rock or Snow, but Benson is astute enough to realise that between 'the well worn track ... and the cragsman's ascent of difficult rocks, there is a great deal of country to be covered'. He adopts his earlier method and takes the reader on a scramble on Eel Crags, pointing out as he goes the difference between appearance and reality, this time not on the map but when viewed from below. The chapter is substantial and deserves to be. It is a feature of climbing in these isles that there are a number of excellent days to be had on good solid rock ridges where care is essential but the rewards are high. The Snowdon Horseshoe, the Aonach Eagach Ridge and the more straightforward parts of the Cuillin all provide an easily accessible opportunity to experience something more exciting than plodding up a grassy slope to reach the summit.

In fact, Benson's proposals are nowhere near as ambitious (Skye is completely out of bounds for all but the most expert) but nevertheless contain some interesting suggestions. One of these is to draw an imaginary straight line from point A to point B and to follow it as closely as possible. In today's traffic this seems an attractive proposition that will take you to places, even in otherwise familiar territory, that you have not visited before. Benson brings to bear his other recreation, hunting with hounds, which in the Lakes is done on foot. As foxes tend to avoid the tourist track and have a good deal of agility, the huntsman has not only to cover rough ground quickly but additionally have a good eye for possible routes when the ground steepens. His first book, *Crag and Hound in Lakeland*, published in 1902, explains in some detail the connection he has found between the two sports.

His treatise on Rock Climbing seems to comprise mainly gullies and chimneys and contains the time-honoured principles of letting the feet do the work, pressing up rather than pulling down and having the confidence to use small intermediary holes. Other-wise it is more to do with rope management than anything else. Much time is spent on the topic and beneath this palimpsest another theme can be faintly traced. The composition of a rope (talented leader at the front, dependable stalwart second and all-too-willing-to-learn-and-obey bringing up the rear) seems to reflect not only his view on good mountaineering practice but also of an ideal society at large—a sort of hemp rope of being, as it were.

But if the introduction had been properly read and digested, it would have been clear that the book has a function other than that of an officers' training manual. The castigation of folly runs as a thread through the volume. The appeal is emotive...

A dear friend of mine ... was accidentally killed on our mountains. The shock of his death was almost immediately fatal to his mother, and though less swift (and less merciful) not less mortal to his sister. Decline set its inexorable hand on her, and, though she lingered for some months, she never rallied. I appeal to you, you young climbers. You are generous humane men ... Do not, I beseech you, in the pursuit of your pastime rashly risk the infliction of such bitter suffering. Accidents must, I fear, sometimes happen. Let it be your business to see that no selfishness of yours is the cause of one.

... yet at times irrational. He has spent much of the book trying to educate the reader into avoiding an accident but his final sentiment is to wish that, like 'a cheeky schoolboy' or 'an officer who has been disgracing his regiment', any impertinent young fellow who breaks the rules of safe mountaineering should be made to take a tumble and thus be taught a salutary lesson. Where those bereft of relatives, military experience or formal education stand in the midst of such turpitude is, however, less than clear.

So what, in Benson's opinion, are these acts of selfishness?

Climbing Alone (the greatest of sins). 'They [the solitary climbers] are worse than the kleptomaniac, who knows it is wrong to steal, yet cannot help stealing; for they know that they are doing wrong, can help it, and still do it.'

Outcrop Climbing. Useful for training, but highly dangerous if it gives a man delusions of grandeur. Excellence as a 'rock-gymnast does not necessarily constitute excellence as a rock climber', as excellence as a rock climber does not necessarily constitute excellence as a mountaineer.

Attempting Exceptionally Severe Courses. As with outcrop climbing, there is a tendency to self-satisfaction, with the added complication that the activity requires a length of run-out that 'exceeds the bounds of legitimate climbing'.

The Graduated List of Climbs. 'In the hands of a sensible sportsman [it] is most valuable; in the hands of a fool [rock-gymnast, etc] it is dangerous.'

Inappropriate Dress. Benson has a special section on Mountaineering for Ladies in which he beseeches them to '*start* neat, at any rate' and not emulate some men who 'seem to glory in a collarless, unshaven, unbrushen, Weary Willie appearance'.

Encouraging Women to Climb. Benson reports that he has been led to believe that they are 'moderately helpless' in the 'art of tieing knots' and that 'a woman who has *once* overwalked herself seems doomed to be more or less of an invalid for life', to such an extent that 'Doctors ... are constantly having girls on their hands who have overdone it, and will never be quite the same again.'

All this paternalism, ridiculous as it appears today, could be justified if at its heart lay the interest of others. But there are too many clues in the text that the truly selfish are the author and those he represents. Early in the introduction he describes the peaks, passes and glaciers as being the 'quarry of [the] chosen few' and extols the 'Band of Brothers' who formed the Alpine Club. To his regret, he realises that this state cannot be preserved in aspic and that outsiders will muscle in: 'enthusiasts daring, but, alas! imprudent and unskilled', who will bring with them not only public censure for their folly but also 'the caterer, the hotel proprietor, the tripper and, worst of all, the lift and funicular railways'.

It is clear that in Benson's mind only those who have served a long apprenticeship 'helplessly tied to the tail of a guide', as Abraham had put it, can consider themselves true mountaineers. Benson trumpets that although he has had the chance to essay the exceptionally difficult courses and considers he has the ability to complete them, albeit as a second, he has not taken up the opportunity. As he explained, 'I might conceivably have set a bad example and that is a risk I would rather not undertake.' A Danish lady's protestations spring to mind.

Benson is into damage limitation. He knows that he cannot stop change but hopes he might influence its direction and to this end he quotes, not once but twice, from an address by Charles Edward Mathews, a former President of the Alpine Club.

It may be that I am only a voice crying in the wilderness, but I implore you, the mountaineers of the future, to do nothing that can discredit our favourite pursuit, or bring down the ridicule of the undiscerning upon the noblest pastime in the world.

Another reason for imagining that Benson felt

obliged to go to print was that George Abraham, a mountaineer of some note, had successfully published a similar manual, *The Complete Mountaineer*, two years earlier. Although this volume made the distinction between the proper ambitions of experts and novices, Benson may have felt it did not lay due emphasis on avoiding 'discredit' and that it was incumbent upon him to set the record straight. Nor could he be sure that a man who made his money out of photographing mountains and mountaineers could, if he were to turn his hand to further publication, be trusted to have the Corinthian principles at heart.

But, whatever its possible shortfall, Abraham's book had every claim to be regarded as 'complete'. No detail is omitted, from the trivial tip of drying your boots by filling them with oats (no doubt converted into porridge at the appropriate later moment) to the more vexed question of 'tipping' Alpine guides. The volume ranges over the suitable techniques to be employed on rock and snow, both in this country and abroad, and provides a full gazetteer as to where they might be employed. Finally, as nothing gives an enterprise more worth than an illustrious history, there is one on 'Mountaineering in England', or rather, the Lake District, or perhaps the hills within striking distance of the Wastdale Inn. In fact, so complete was the undertaking that within three months of publication a second edition appeared.

Once the various techniques have been described, which interestingly enough for 1907 include the art of hand-jamming, there is a section on the dangers of mountaineering which ends with twenty-one rules of what should and should not be done. This is not as preachy as it sounds and is based on straightforward common sense, clearly expressed, rather than with the emotional quiver that Benson adopts when trying to persuade his readers to the straight and narrow path of moral responsibility. The admonition, when felt necessary, is more subtle and a warning on the dangers, for example, of underrating a climb comes by way of a light-hearted anecdote. Abraham recalls an entry in the Wastdale visitors book which read 'Ascended the Pillar Rock in three hours and found the rocks very easy.' Inscribed immediately below was the riposte, 'Descended the Pillar Rock in three seconds, and found the rocks very hard.'

Some thirty-odd years later, another book of instruction was to appear which took matters a stage further. Written by Colin Kirkus, the foremost climber of his day, *Let's Go Climbing* was part of a series aimed at young readers in the hope of persuading them to take up a particular sport or pastime. Kirkus had clearly studied his brief as carefully as he had the photographs of Clogwyn Du'r Arddu which he famously kept secreted in the drawer of his office desk. He realised that if he were to succeed in this task he had to catch the attention of his audience as quickly as possible and, once this was engaged, to work hard to maintain interest.

He knew that youth is more likely to be caught up with the particular than the general and, moreover, that the particular must have some sort of edge. The best bet, he decided, was to recount his own early experiences, warts and all, and let the readers decide for themselves. The simplest way to lose the attention of children is to treat them like children, so Kirkus employs different tactics. Within a few pages of the start, he has taken his readers into his confidence. He stresses the importance of training your parents from an early age, otherwise they tend to interfere. He had found from his own experience that, if properly managed, they gave little trouble. Benson at this stage was probably shifting uneasily in his grave.

The opening chapter entitled 'Why Do We Climb?' sets out to answer the question, not through philosophic speculation but with an example which Kirkus hopes will capture the imagination. He describes a winter night's climb to the top of Snowdon, starting from the Ogwen Valley. It's all there, the moonlight dazzling on the snow, the patches of shadow to confuse the unwary, the climber creeping over the walls of the Pen-y-Pass Hotel at three in the morning with the skill of a cat-burglar, then crossing the pinnacles of Cribs Goch and y Ddysgl to the top of Yr Wyddfa.

There is a sense of real excitement as the story unfolds. The spur-of-the-moment decision to embark on a midnight adventure, discovery threatened by the clatter of nailed boots on a frozen road, the beautiful dangers of the ice-bound Snowdon ridges all accord with the young's idea of meaningful enterprise. Then, after spending a shivering night in what remained of the summit hut, he and they are given the reward of a perfect sunrise and a sweltering descent into the snow-filled bowl of Glaslyn.

Of course, it could be argued that a number of cardinal sins had been committed. Going out alone after a hard day's climbing, not leaving notice of his plans, tackling ice-covered ridges without rope or companion would have been seen as foolhardy by some, not least by the now gyroscopic Benson. But the point that Kirkus makes is that the adventure is worth the risk and the risk is worth taking, provided you can manage it properly.

Nevertheless, the dangers that face the beginner must be identified and warned against, which usually means the raising of an admonitory finger. Kirkus avoids the stance of adult superiority which he has been eager to dispel by holding up his own early follies as examples of what is to be avoided. As he knew no one who climbed and so could advise him, he was forced to find out for himself. Armed only with Abraham's *British Mountain Climbs*, he set off to attempt his first proper route. This was Arch Gully on Craig yr Isfa and as it was described as 'Difficult' Kirkus approached it with some apprehension. All went well, however, and elated he turned his attention to the harder B Gully in the back of the Amphitheatre. Technically, it required more care and thought than his bull-in-a-china-shop approach and not once but twice he finished in a heap at the bottom of the pitch. As the second fall had taken him to the edge of a rather nasty drop, he realised that there are times when discretion is the better part of valour. This late admission of his guilty secret only adds to the sense of conspiracy that he is trying to establish.

Frightening experiences, again solo, on Javelin Gully and while prospecting a new route on Craig Lloer were central to his own climbing education. The lesson that over-confidence, inexperience and lack of judgment could and should be replaced with calm and forethought thus passes effortlessly to the reader. The whole section is neatly balanced between The Ripping Yarn and The Cautionary Tale and demonstrates the ultimate teaching skill of simultaneously enthusing yet advising. But what is particularly interesting to note is the amount of actual information that the piece imparts without descending to lecture level. By the end of the chapter, the reader has been taught about the various types of climb that may be encountered and the techniques that might be employed to overcome them. In addition, there is an explanation of the various terms that real climbers use. But all this is so seamlessly done that there is no sense that you are enduring a geography lesson

There are occasions when specific instruction is necessary and the Kirkus method of teaching mountain navigation is, interestingly enough, very similar in method to the one employed by Benson. Both take a map of a suitable area and invite the tyro to navigate a theoretical route across the hills. Similar in method but not in manner. There is a sense of smugness when Benson, having placed his guinea pig 'metaphorically' on the top of Grasmoor with instructions to get home safely, tells how his student decided to walk over the edge of a cliff. Kirkus also points out the danger of navigational error but his tone is more sympathetic and I am sure that Benson's expression 'that it behoved [him] to do what in [him] lay to try to point out what may, and what may not, be learned from an ordinary map of a British mountain group', were not the words Kirkus would have used to emphasise his own sense of responsibility.

It might now be interesting to look back at Benson's catalogue of selfish behaviour and see how the new man measures up.

Climbing Alone. Although Kirkus explains the possible dangers, he believes that it teaches judgment and self-reliance. Indeed, as the whole point of climbing is, in his opinion, leading and, if possible, leading new routes, the ability to climb up and down without depending on a rope is a prerequisite.

Outcrop Climbing. Surprisingly, he agrees with Benson on this point, believing it better for the beginner to savour the whole of the mountain experience rather than concentrating on gymnastics. However, he disagrees on its ultimate value, regarding gritstone problems as an advanced course to be undertaken once the basics have been mastered.

Attempting Exceptionally Severe Courses. One chapter is devoted to his first ascent of the Great Slab on Cloggy, a route which, with its long run-outs and lack of protection, would certainly exceed Benson's 'bounds of legitimate climbing'. Not only does Kirkus enthuse over his plunge into the unknown but also, by implication, encourages his readers to follow his example.

The Graduated List of Climbs. He built his climbing career around just such lists.

Inappropriate Dress. Kirkus advises that any old clothes will do and emphasises practicality rather than sartorial elegance.

Encouraging Women to Climb. He specifically states that his remarks are meant for girls as much as boys, even to the extent of advising them to borrow their brothers' trousers as suitably appropriate wear.

He also draws attention to the Pinnacle Club and Dorothy Pilley's *Climbing Days* as particular sources of inspiration. There is still the air of male condescension that you might expect in 1941 but it is a far cry from the prognosis of Benson's medical friends.

After the war, climbing seeped into the educative process. Instruction manuals appeared but, like rationing and coupons, they bore the label of utility rather than adventure and reflected the bureaucracy that was soon to surround the sport. In these days of drop-of-the-hat litigation and Certificated Mountain Leaders, the views of even conservative Victorians, whose concept of arresting a falling leader was to hurl oneself over the opposite side of the ridge, would seem cavalier. As for the suggestion of a book that proposes that children should ignore their elders and betters, abandon the safety of the 4x4 and find out about life for themselves, most present-day publishers would assume it was meant as some sort of a joke.

The Good, the Bad and the Angry

Outside what is generally known as mountaineering literature lies a collection of writing which is usually significant and often distinguished. Much of this is to be found in the journals of the various climbing clubs which, in providing the facility and structuring the traditions, shaped the nature of the sport. These compilations of the doings of the club may be regarded as the 'good', if only as an acknowledgment of the selfless efforts of the various editors who ensured a record of the club's activities and continued to foster the band of brotherism that is essential to any group of consenting adults mutually involved in an eccentric activity.

It is interesting to speculate whether, without such support, climbing as a formalised sport would have existed at all. A man, if he so wishes, can stand at the bottom of a cliff and, without reference to any outside source, climb to its top by any means he chooses and that is that. But once he returns to the valley and writes up his experience for others to read, then matters change. He is now suggesting a framework which the said others can either adopt or challenge and what has, up to that point, been essentially an individual experience can quickly become a challenging benchmark for others to eye.

The club journal is the logical extension of such hotel or hut log-books. But the editorial process triggers a subtle distinction, or rather addition. An individual who might be loth to parade his achievements for their own sake might be persuaded to do so for the benefit of others. Moreover, the editor can insert a critical judgment suggesting that Way A is more sporting than Way B. When the Abrahams named their route on Pillar the New West Route, they knowingly implied that it was in some way different from—that is, more challenging than—the Old West first climbed by a local shepherd, John Atkinson. So standards can be set and targets identified. The journal, of course, may contain other items to amuse or entertain but the main thrust, at least in its beginnings, was to lay out the field of play.

The first volume of the Fell & Rock Journal, the three issues of which cover the years 1907-1909, illustrates the point. There is, of necessity, the usual paraphernalia of club conviviality and bureaucratic democracy but the majority of the articles are about the climbs in the district and how to accomplish them. It does not take long for a level of governance to appear, instructing members in climbing method, and by the third issue an ex-President feels free to thunder on the evils of '(i) competitive climbing; (ii) lack of appreciation of the difficulties and dangers; and (iii) tackling difficult climbs with chance companions'. More significantly, his piece has an epigraph which informs the members that the article 'has the sanction of the club's executive, and must be regarded as its official expression with regard to the matters it discusses'.

So, the simple wanderings of a shepherd were transformed into a sport which, as all sports do, laid down in the appropriate tablets exactly where to do it, how to do it and, most importantly, how to behave while doing it.

But out of this original 'good' sprang a 'bad': the guidebook. At least, it was thought 'bad' in certain quarters. The objection was that a detailed account of where the climber should go and what difficulties he might expect undermined the very nature of the sport. As Geoffrey Winthrop Young, spokesman for the Climbers' Club, explained, 'the Matterhorn is unchangeably the Matterhorn for all the hundred who trample up and down it ... We only have to avoid them, or to learn merely to shut them out of our mind's eye and the sublimity meets us unaltered'–i.e. in the absence of contrary evidence we can pretend every ascent is a first ascent. The giveaway is, of course, the use of the first person. The mountains belong to the chosen few, the hand-picked, to whom the delights of the likes of Lliwedd would be dispensed so they too could experience 'the lift of its sombre precipice above the ruffled lake' and reincarnate 'the mystery and uncertainty and all of the delight that it held for those who first ventured upon it'.

In fact, the Climbers' Club, London-based and steeped in Alpine tradition, had a far wider agenda than reducing the rock faces of Britain to a series of eliminates. The parties that gathered at Pen-y-Pass were essentially a social gathering. People were invited for themselves, rather than their climbing ability. In order that all could be equally involved, ropes were arranged so that the strong helped the weak. There were, of course, the stars, a Mallory, Pope or Herford who might linger after the main party had dispersed, whereon a new crag might be discovered or a further girdle flung. But competition, *per se*, was frowned upon. As with that other emerging social enterprise, Rugby Football, you might enquire as to which Club your acquaintance belonged but never at which level of competence he was normally selected.

There was, perhaps, another reason for the upturned nose. The only existing publication which produced a detailed account of existing routes had appeared in 1897. It was the unequivocally entitled *Rock Climbing in the English Lake District,* written by the foremost climber of his generation, Owen Glynne Jones. Although that guide was discursive and generously sprinkled with anecdote, there is little doubt of its intention and that was to give the reader a detailed understanding of the nature and difficulty of the climbs described. Of the 'And lo! the Hunter of the East has caught the cliffs of Lliwedd' school, it was not. Moreover, the climbs were not only graded into the categories Easy, Moderate, Difficult and Exceptionally Severe but they were ranked in order of difficulty within the grades. To those who saw mountaineering as a sublime, even mystical, experience, this shopkeepers' catalogue must have seemed an anathema. It must have confirmed their worst fears that if commercialism set in, the chara-bancs would inevitably follow.

What was worse, it was republished by the Abraham brothers, and the Abrahams, professional photographers and publishers, were 'trade'. Their concern was more about money than mystery and they had no wish to keep the mountains to themselves. As their note prefacing the second edition of Jones' opus states, 'The rapid exhaustion of the first edition … and further numerous enquiries for copies of this unique and invaluable work, induced us to make arrangements for the publication of another issue.' The key as to the real motive is an appendix that includes climbs completed after Jones' death. It is clear that the intention was not simply to reproduce the work in memory of their old friend but to put into place an ongoing commercial proposition that cashed in on climbing developments within the district.

Nor was the Climbers' Club the only voice to be raised against such acts of sacrilege. The Scottish Mountaineering Club had similar reservations about its own patch but these may have been more prag-matically based. The only time that the Highlands could more or less be guaranteed to be free from snow coincided with the garnering season for the various ingredients of game pie and at such a time the climber was not welcome. At all other times the difficulty of any route would be entirely dependent on the conditions and any attempt to give more than a general outline would be pointless. The best way to tackle any gully, ridge or buttress would depend on circumstance rather than previous exploration.

All would have been well for the likes of Winthrop Young if only future guidebooks had limited their ambition to the 'small, amiable' volumes of *Climbing in the British Isles* by W P Haskett Smith, published in 1894. These had little connection with the plastic-covered oracles of today. In common with many Victorians intent on research, Haskett Smith felt the need to catalogue rather than randomly list. Matters should be ordered by magnitude, genus, etc, but, if all else failed, alphabetically. So the first real description of climbing in England starts with Alum Pot, swerves eccentrically through the importance of Clapham, a station on the Midland Railway, as an excellent centre for Ingleborough, the etymology surrounding Eel Crag and a variety of Shamrocks, before landing safely in the ridings of Yorkshire.

Amongst all this detail, however, lies an account of the climbs available to the would-be mountaineer and, as Haskett Smith explains in his introduction, this is the rationale for the book itself: 'Many might-be mountaineers ... did not become Alpine because they were afraid that they should make fools of themselves if they went on the Alps.' If, he went on, they had only known, they could have practised at home in the same way that the would-be skater uses the little pond at the end of the garden 'where early flounderings would be safe from the contemptuous glances of unsympathetic experts'.

No challenge was beneath his dignity. Not Bear Rock, 'a queerly-shaped rock on *Great Napes* [that] is a little difficult to find ... when the grass is at all long' nor Eight-Foot Drop, a closely identified variation on an earlier variation of a rather obscure route on the East Face of Pillar Rock. Nor was he bound by the conventions of his contemporaries who saw climbing in Britain as only worthwhile if it prepared them for their greater struggles in the Alps. As his ascent and descent of Napes Needle show, he had an eye for the rock problem *per se* and his section on English climbing was by no means confined to the Lake District. The tors of Dartmoor and the limestone cliffs of Malham Cove and Gordale Scar are assessed as possible climbing venues. What is more, there is a surprisingly modern view of sea cliff climbing, with a discussion of the merits of Beachy Head and, in the companion volumes concerning Wales and Ireland, an acknowledgment of the possibilities on Anglesey and Fairhead, the northern promontory of County Antrim.

The writing reflects the man. Always self-deprecating—his description of the Needle, although at pains to name those who made the second, third and fourth ascents and the first ascent by a lady, makes no reference to his own endeavour—he nevertheless keeps a wry eye on any over-inflated opinion of others. The description of Plynlimon in *The Beauties of Wales* (1813) as a 'towering summit' makes Haskett Smith wonder whether the writer had ever been near the place. He notes that Pennant, on the other hand, candidly admitted (1770) that he never saw it, 'which is easily understood, for the mountain is neither easy to see nor worth looking at when seen. The ascent is a protracted bog-walk.'

He was also of his time and type. Educated at Eton and Trinity, he was the sort of man who would expect to have a private ice-rink at the bottom of his garden. Although he qualified as a barrister, he never considered this as an opportunity for financial reward. In fact, he once had a furious row with a solicitor friend who had the temerity to send him a brief. Instead, armed with his Ordnance Survey maps, he trawled the countryside, noting and no doubt attempting to climb up and down the various crests and troughs he encountered. One possible explanation for this surprising variety, if not plethora, of physical phenomena is that, according to his obituarist in the Fell & Rock Journal, the 'father of British climbing' was quite likely, even on the simplest of walks, to lose his way.

Unlike Jones, Haskett Smith made no attempt to grade the climbs but rather counted on his readers' knowledge of the ability and reputation of the pioneers to form a judgment of the difficulties involved. For example, in his description of the Great Gully on the Wastwater Screes, he quotes Dr Collie's account of the first ascent, which had appeared in the Scottish Mountaineering Club Journal. Collie recalls the struggle on the last pitch:

Robinson and I afterwards ascended this formidable place by means of the moral support of the rope alone. But I know that in my case, if that moral

support had not been capable of standing the strain
... I should probably have been spoiling a patch of
snow several hundreds of feet lower down the gill.

The implication was clear. If as eminent a climber as Collie required the assistance of the rope, this was no place for a novice. This method of explanation by inference worked well if all parties involved were on the same wavelength but was potentially disastrous for those less well versed in ironic understatement.

It was this lack of unequivocal information on the difficulties involved that eventually led the doyen of the Climbers' Club to authorise the official version which detailed the rock climbs in North Wales. It was agreed that the guidebook would overstate rather than understate and clearly identify the nature and extent of the difficulties, and this format quickly became the norm. At least, until the production of the long-awaited Cloggy guide in 1963, when a perusal of the personnel featuring in the List of First Ascents, with the accompanying laconic comments ('It rained, so the second did not follow.') told you more about the nature of the climb than any description, adjectival or otherwise. As one reviewer put it:

While according to Hughie may well be phooey,
According to Crew is true.

Meanwhile, Haskett Smith was understandably oblivious to the forthcoming furore and set about producing similar accounts for Wales and, enlisting the help of H C Hart, Ireland. A survey of Scotland was part of the original plan but was respectfully abandoned when he discovered the Scottish Mountaineering Club intended a comprehensive review of its own. The exploration of Wales differs in tone from the English section. The pervading theme is one of gloom. As Jim Perrin observes in his entertaining introduction to the facsimile edition published by the Ernest Press in 1986, 'The very first entry sets the tone with accounts of three fatalities and a serious injury at Aber Falls, and from there on the carnage scarcely lets up until the end of the volume.'

In fact, the invasion of the tourist seems by now to have filled even Haskett Smith with as much alarm as his successors. Good road and rail links made the mountains of North Wales more accessible than the Lake District and the surrounding cities seemed only too willing to provide the necessary sacrificial victims for the resident Afanc. After the demise of one George Henry Frodsham, a clerk from Liverpool who, encumbered by a variety of impedimenta, lost his way and fell to his death on Snowdon, the author remarks, 'It may be said that the party neglected no precaution which is likely to ensure a fatal accident– inexperience, fatigue, darkness, difficult rocks, the burden of bags and umbrellas.'

So it was only a matter of time before J M A Thomson's guidebooks, at the behest of the Climbers' Club, duly appeared. The first, in conjunction with A W Andrews, describing the cliffs of Lliwedd, was unveiled in 1909, to be followed by a solo effort in 1910 entitled *Climbing in the Ogwen District.* These can be regarded as the first rock climbing guidebooks. They differ from Jones' volume, which is really a series of articles drawn from his own experience. Thomson's descriptions are more objective and clearly designed to assist the climber to complete in safety the route in question. As well as a general assessment of difficulty, there is a step-by-step account of each section (or pitch) of the climb and within the description there is advice, often detailed and specific, as to the best way of tackling the problem. In other words, he laid down a blueprint for those that followed. The only significant addition that his successors made was to give the length of individual pitches, rather than maximum length of rope required overall.

But if Thomson was meticulous, then one of those successors in Snowdonia could reasonably be described as cavalier. Menlove Edwards, in the 1930s, undertook a review of much of the climbing in the district. The first of these, in conjunction with Wilfred Noyce, was again Lliwedd. It was completed in record time by dint of climbing thousands of feet a day during an extended camping holiday. If the original guide was deliberately conservative in that it overstated the difficulties, Edwards redressed the balance by grading most of the harder climbs as more or less V Diff. Even Avalanche Route, originally described as 'the most exposed climb in England and Wales ... only for a thoroughly expert party', was reduced to 'a very open route of no special difficulty but of obvious charm and sufficiently steady to keep the interest going'.

The reason for this iconoclasm is uncertain. The uniform nature of the cliff and continually climbing at a standard where the authors were rarely stretched may have made them think that the routes were much of a muchness. And there is no doubt that Edwards was irritated by the adjectival method of grading that threw up such linguistic absurdities as Easy Difficult and Mild Severe. His description in the Cwm Idwal guide of the Ordinary Route on the Slabs as 'Moderately Easy with a few feet Moderately Difficult', where the modifier takes two opposed meanings in the same sentence, was no doubt used to underline his point. His preferred method was a numerical rank from 1–6 that reflected the technical difficulty, accompanied by a literary description that examined the objective dangers and the overall seriousness of the climb. However, the Establishment that had just become used to the Shopkeepers' Catalogue jibbed at the idea of a Periodic Table. So we will never know what he had in mind as to the range of suitable warnings on the objective danger of a leader accidentally departing the rock face. It probably ran from 'Likely to cause a variety of damage if the second is paying insufficient attention' to 'Extremely calamitous to all concerned'.

If the guide to Lliwedd had been tempered by the views of a co-author, there was no such restriction when Edwards turned his attention to Cwm Idwal. Impatient with the lack of ambition shown by most climbers, he remarks of the Ordinary Route, 'It soon took upon itself the mantle of prosperity and its repute flourished', followed by 'A good route for beginners with an ineptitude for steep places'. He underlined his point by describing a series of climbs he had recently completed on Clogwyn y Geifr, a precipice surrounding the Devil's Kitchen, which for a variety of superstitious reasons had been regarded as unjustifiably dangerous. Whilst not quite adopting the approach of his article in the Climbers' Club Journal—

It has every natural advantage, being steep, composed of pretty rocky sort of rock and being covered with vegetation ... It is not of course the cliff for those who attack the problem tooth and nail nor yet for those who rise by seizing every opportunity, but I think it may be now considered safe for democracy. It is years since anybody was killed there.

—he nevertheless broke from the norm. It was, after all, his cliff. First, he decided to dispense with the higher grades of Hard and Very Severe, 'owing to the difficulty of technical comparison with the grass, bad rock and the immaturity of these climbs'. Second, his particular description of the route did not follow the accepted format. Edwards objected to the 'spotlight' approach that the Fell & Rock had developed, where you might have a precise idea of where you were in conjunction with the hold you had just left and the hold you were about to grasp, but no sense as to where you were on the cliff as a whole. He also wanted to give a feel of the climb so that the climber is able to 'pick out what climb will suit what mood or preference'. A few examples will suffice to give the flavour.

Hothouse Crack. It is neither much exposed nor much enclosed, and the level is kept up. It is full of a large variety of flowering plants which all show most luxuriant growth.

Devil's Dump. The resemblance to a Dump is remarkable, and is due to the prevalence of various types of herbage, the projections of agglomerate on the steep section, and to the general melancholy appearance.

Devil's Buttress. The ground is very grassy and anxiety is thus saved as to the rock, which is poor.

Cellar Buttress. The main features are grass, bad rock and progressive difficulty ... It is nowhere hard.

The whole affair is summed up by the prefatory comment, 'Experience in grass and bad rock, if not gained before, is likely to be early fostered on Clogwyn y Geirf.'

Needless to say, succeeding guidebooks dispensed with much of this additional material and adopted a mode of sensible responsibility, which is no doubt a good thing for people who take their climbing seriously. Nevertheless

While according to Crew may well be true,
The odd effervescent is pleasant.

Then guidebooks fell, if not out of fashion, at least out of print. Standards had risen, not through the efforts of the few, whose deeds of daring could be divided and passed amongst the chosen, but as a statistical outcome of the increase in participants. Guidebooks simply could not keep up. Borrowdale was a good example. In 1960, when the latest Fell & Rock guide was reprinted, there were a couple of dozen routes graded VS and these included such notables as Abraham's finish to Mouse Ghyll, put up in 1897. By 1966, when the rogue *Borrowdale, A Climber's Guide* by Ross and Thompson appeared, the number of climbs included at that grade and above had increased by more than a hundred, a pattern that was being replicated across the country.

This offered an ideal opportunity for the commercial world to step in. 1962 saw the appearance of *The Climber* on the bookstalls and those, the vast majority, who did not have access to the journals of the established clubs gleaned what they could from its contents. It was not only new climbs but also new crags that were being reported and I still have some-where, in a box marked 'Things not to be thrown away', a variety of cuttings of crags, natural and man-made, that are scattered around the Pennine chain. There was the usual commercial overtone, explaining the advantageous use of Scandinavian compasses and cooking utensils, but it was reader-friendly and even, if I remember rightly, published readers' poems. At any rate, this particular magazine seemed to be of more use than the official organ of the BMC which appeared, for the most part, to con-sist of diagrams based on an A Level syllabus for Quantum Mechanics.

But then came the Great Gear Explosion. Whereas previously it had been the norm to assail the cliffs in cast-off gardening trousers and cut-down pacamacs, now science stepped in. Various fabrics, each one more magical than the last, appeared in a diversity of hue and were dangled before the eyes of full employment and credit cards. Rusting nuts scavenged from the foundry floor were replaced by shiny metal cuboids. Slippers, excruciatingly pain-ful but with the sticking power of a gecko, promised the stuff that dreams were made of. And it was not long before the proprietors realised that the mass market was walkers and what was really needed were Bumper Boot Guides. *The Climber* embraced the *Rambler*. There were articles and diagrams as to where the bumper boots could be guided and useful hints like how to avoid sunburn. The overall impression was of a comfortable merry-go-round rather than a determined effort to reflect the concerns of the average hill-goer.

In 1991, however, a blow was stuck. *The Angry Corrie*, a hill fanzine, appeared on the market. Edited by Dave Hewitt and Perkin Warbeck (aka Doug Small), its intention was to make waves rather than a profit and, according to the first edition, adopt 'radically outspoken standpoints wherever necessary and (more importantly) by the trusty old medium of humour'. 'The totally useless equipment guide No 1: The map case' sets the tone. As does 'Meet the authors ...', a series of pen-portraits of the great and the good in the Scottish mountain literary scene, none of whom made or, given the content, is likely to make any contribution to the first or future editions.

The template was the football fanzine, a type of publication that has proliferated in response to the self-indulgent behaviour of bored millionaire owners, overpaid players and inconsiderate media demands. In Hewitt's case, the football was Scottish and that meant Glaswegian and as a result *TAC*'s house style resembles more a Saturday night pub argument than the South Bank Show. The upshot is somewhere between *Private Eye* and *Viz*, though the editors would prefer to be grouped with the latter. It is therefore probably no coincidence that I first came across the publication in a dingy corner shop that seemed to be making its livelihood through selling Bovril-stained match programmes and an assortment of somewhat arcane comics.

TAC is for the most part unchanged over fifteen years, with a regular group of contributors and a circulation of around 1000 per issue, so there is a danger that it will, or even has, become a merry-go-round within a merry-go-round. It, like any small publisher, will point to the problems of distribution (Hewitt set up a pitch on Beinn Narnain to help launch the first issue) but the time might be right for a fresh push. A potential readership might by now have caught up with the originators' vision. People are today less likely to be taken in by the glossy sales talk of the nineties and have started to realise that the movers and shakers have a somewhat selfish waddle of their own.

The emergence of FC United is a case in point. This breakaway group of fans, fed up with the way their team was being reduced to a marketing tool, launched their own version of what they wanted Man Utd to be (traditional strips, no advertising logos, etc). The club is working its way through the divisions, attracting, much to the delight of local treasurers, several thousand real fans, as opposed to effete southerners. (*TAC* equivalent of the latter is English Munro-baggers.)

Of course, it is easier to channel enthusiasm into a sport, which has easily recognised goals, than it is into a pastime. Hill-goers have no equivalent of FC United's immediate ambition to reach the level where they would be eligible to play Man Utd in the FA Cup. But it would only be petty change for a oil billionaire to fund the distribution of free copies of *TAC* to every climbing outlet in the UK, with a call to arms to all those who value the hills as they are and not as some self-appointed improvement scheme would have them.

Stranger than Fact

Serious fiction and mountain writing make uneasy bedfellows. It is too tempting for an author to seize upon the inevitable moments of crisis and press the melodrama button. Crumbling rocks, slipping fingers and severed ropes can easily become the staple diet to feed plot or shape character. To anyone who has actually been in such situations, the contortions can quickly become more irritating than entertaining.

The dangers were spotted at an early stage. In 1915 C F Holland posted an article from the Western Front to the editor of the Fell & Rock Journal. It was entitled 'Another Climbing Story: A MS from "Somewhere in France"' and in it he relates a recent experience. Returning from duty at a local farm, which had consisted of 'guarding sundry articles, mainly broken spades', he attempted to make himself comfortable on a bed of ammunition boxes. For reasons not specified, sleep failed him and as compensation he found himself leafing through a discarded magazine where he was 'charmed to find' a story based on the exploits of a climbing expedition. As a member of the party which had recently succeeded on the first ascent of the Central Buttress of Scafell, then reputed to be one of the most difficult climbs in the world, he naturally read on with interest.

The gist of the matter (and Holland assures us that his account is as accurate as he could possibly make it) was that a party of five, one guide, two men (of whom one was the hero) and two women (of whom one was the heroine) were attempting a route in the Rockies. Matters started to accelerate when the party (roped together at twelve-foot intervals) found themselves on a steep slab, which ended in a fathomless abyss.

There are no holds. What to do? Obvious solution of difficulty—to slide. The guide slides, the hero slides, they all slide, the guide first because he is leading, the heroine last because she is the weak member of the party.

However, the heroine's sliding lacks the proper technique and she is about to plunge over the edge when her leg is caught in the nick of time by the hero. This thoroughly modern miss, far from being grateful, berates the hero for his 'too masterful' attitude. The plot thickens. The rope takes on a mind of its own and does everything in its power to bring ruin upon the expedition, in particular looping around convenient bollards of rock. But the heroine is up to its tricks and every crafty twist and turn it can muster she duly thwarts. In the end, the rope has had enough and decides to do her in.

A second time it is foiled, this time by the hero, who again seizes the heroine, by the leg, who is thus saved from being thrown over another precipice by the now thoroughly infuriated rope.

'We breathe again'—but the rope is not to be thwarted and severs itself against a conveniently sharp piece of rock. The hero and heroine are marooned. There follows a further suffragette moment when the heroine insists on taking the lead and is only prevented by the hero yet again grasping her leg and yet again saving her from her own folly. At last, through a hail of falling rocks and sliding shale (over further fathomless abysses), it seem that they will reach the top, only to be repulsed by a holdless slab. At which point the hero breaks down and weeps. This has the effect of causing the heroine to profess her undying love, a proposition which, under the circumstances, seems a tad optimistic.

It was at this point that Holland paused to contemplate how the inevitable nuptial campanology was to be achieved. Possible solutions included an airman dangling a rope which the hero, heroine clasped in arms, would grab by the teeth, or a sudden reversal of gravity whereupon they are swept up to the summit on an avalanche. The actuality is disappointingly prosaic. The guide reappears and points out some 'invisible crevices' which make the problem several grades easier than the Ordinary Route on Idwal Slabs.

Even if the writer exercises considerably greater restraint than the author of Holland's topographically bemused manuscript, the problem still has to be faced that fiction of this type can carry less impact than fact. The publication of Joe Simpson's real-life struggle in *Touching the Void* has surely put paid to any future Man against Mountain novel. But there is room for a novel which is about climbing as it actually is, rather than as it is popularly perceived. Perhaps the best known example is Elizabeth Coxhead's *One Green Bottle*, in which the heroine, Cathy Canning, escapes from the slums of Merseyside to discover herself and the wider horizons of life in the pleasures of rock climbing.

On the surface, the story appears to be a fable that illustrates the working-class struggle for social justice. Cathy can only escape to North Wales if her income is not required to feed the family. This depends on whether her father is in work, which in turn depends upon the whim of an Argentinian shipping magnate who may or may not place an order with the local shipyard. The novel has been seen as a precursor to those of the likes of Alan Sillitoe, but the book's economic dynamic is rooted more in the attitudes of the Thirties Depression than post-war Keynesian full employment. It is really more about the constraints that marriage places on women of any class and how Cathy, Gwen and Dorothy, respectively, try to cope with their particular problems. In doing so, the narrative produces a feminist twist to the long-debated question as to whether it is nobler in the mind to fulfil one's personal ambition or accede to the expectations of others. Economic circumstance, like the conventions of medieval Denmark, merely gives credibility to the plot.

The novel produced widely different reactions. The renowned educationalist and climber Jack Longland thought it 'by far the best novel about climbing'. Whereas the Bishop of Chester condemned it for its overt sexuality, objecting not only to the fact that the heroine traded in her virginity for a pair of climbing boots but, worse, practised contraception outside marriage. Perhaps 1951 was the point when the Church and the Educational Establishment started to part company.

A far more interesting reaction was expressed by Wilfred Noyce, who suggested that 'it started a new direction in mountain writing', and the direction that he may have had in mind was that *One Green Bottle* is not so much a climbing story as a climber's story. A string of climbs laces its way through the tale and acts as an analogue to Cathy's social, emotional and intellectual development. As she becomes more assured, so the climbs become more challenging. As she relies less on others, so she leads rather than allowing herself to be led.

Moreover, the terms commonly found in a guidebook to indicate the nature of a climb—delicate, awkward, exposed, bold, etc—can be equally applied to everyday situations, and the fundamental grades of Easy, Difficult and Severe can act as modifiers to a human dilemma as well as a rock face. As with all games, climbing can be seen as life writ small. Varying pitches require various techniques, learnt through experience. Stances are moments of calm where stock can be taken and plans made. But Coxhead is writing a novel, not some psychobabble treatise, and she has to make the connections in a way that is both unobtrusive yet consistently credible, particularly to the informed reader. The initial problem is to get the girl from Tooley Street involved in what was, at the time, essentially a middle-class activity.

To add to the difficulty, the climbs that were going to have this formative effect would only become possible if Cathy had the wit and/or luck to acquire a pair of properly nailed boots. She might have been able to cobble together enough old clothing to keep the elements at bay, but a pair of 'hand-made Lawries' would have been far beyond her means. Second, she had to meet up with some real climbers to show her the way. The event that so shocked the Bishop of Chester provided the former, the Ordinary Route on Idwal Slabs the latter.

As part of the weekend deal in Llandudno, the provider of the boots has promised to take Cathy climbing. However, the weather is such that he does not fancy leading and, leaving Cathy to her own resources, tags on to the end of another rope. Cathy, bored, tries the first few feet of Hope, the climb up which they have just disappeared. The combination of balance and movement is too much for her and she soon slithers to the ground. She then spies the furrow that starts the Ordinary Route and steps into what will become an inevitable trap.

Technically straightforward and more gully than crack, the route offers good handholds and a sense of security. But at the crucial moment the fissure closes and the climber is forced for a move or two out into the open. Cathy, remembering her earlier experience of such difficulties, is unwilling to continue and unable to retreat. The good bishop is no doubt rubbing his hands at this point in anticipation of the downward plunge that would so aptly reflect her moral decline. But God works in mysterious ways and her cries for help are not only heard but also deliver her into the arms of Harry and Stan, the most competent and kindly climbers in the valley. This in turn leads her to the Youth Hostel at Cae Capel and its earth-mother warden Dorothy. These introductions, with the accompanying encouragement and advice, kick-start the novel and eventually give it its shape.

An immediate consequence is that Cathy changes her job so that she can leave Birkenhead on Friday night. This means a loss of income and resultant family fury but doubles the amount of time for climbing and, more importantly, the early start means she can join the others on the big mountain expeditions rather than skulking in the valley awaiting their return. The climb chosen to exemplify this advantage is a composite of various routes on Tryfan. At 600 feet long, it offers the perfect introduction to rock climbing as part of mountaineering. It has technically interesting pitches to test the novice, which once mastered will lead to the very summit. The symbolism, though carefully understated, is sufficiently clear to alert the reader to the role that the various climbs play in the remainder of the book.

Once the basics are mastered, it is only a question of time before Cathy starts to lead. The author's choice is again significant as it nudges into the novel's frame one of its more important themes: the role of women in a male-dominated world. Amphitheatre Buttress, as a first lead, is a climb that would have found approval from her male mentors. It is well protected and if a novitiate leader got into difficulties it would be easy enough for them, the support team, to effect a rescue. Cathy has other ideas. In a blow for female equality, she blackmails Dorothy into climbing with her without letting the others know. The next described lead, that of Avalanche on Lliwedd, advances the idea. The nature of the climb, with its poor protection and longish run-outs, means that although Harry and Stan are present, she is effectively on her own, independent of any male assistance. She is their equal. She is in control. Once this has been established, she is quite content to follow Johnny Hollinger, the local tiger, up Great Slab on Cloggy, not because he is a man but because he is the better climber.

But not all her judgments are that sound. Control is a form of power and as such is open to abuse. In an act of retaliation, she deliberately tries to humiliate Dorothy's fiancé. Pressured into taking him climbing, she chooses The Chasm Route on Glyder Fach, fully conscious that the pitch known as the Vertical Vice would prove extremely trying for a novice. Her motives are understandable, as Michael Derwent has gone out of his way to patronise her work in the laundry but, as with all acts of spite, not excusable. It almost goes badly wrong and the lessons learnt may well have had a bearing on her decision at the end of the novel.

Other mountain incidents add texture to this particular pilgrim's progress. Getting lost in the mist after storming out of the hostel in a fit of pique, the near fatal accident to her perceived rival Doreen Lord and guiding a group of deprived schoolchildren over Crib Goch are all epiphanal moments. Perhaps the most telling is on a further ascent of Amphitheatre Buttress. On this occasion Cathy is leading Christopher Thwaites, with whom she will fall in love. They pause on a ledge where she has a view of Johnny leading Harry and Stan up a hard new climb on Amphitheatre Wall. The choice is symbolically laid before her: worthy domesticity married to a schoolteacher or the freedom and satisfaction offered by devoting her life to climbing.

The final climb to be described seems to indicate that the choice has been made. Christopher has been allowed to leave the scene without any real struggle on Cathy's part and she has persuaded Harry to second her on Great Slab. In fact, Harry is really redundant. The nature of the climb and the length of the run-outs mean that it is highly unlikely that a falling leader would have been held. Encouraged by her friends, Cathy climbs with increasing confidence and soon the novel's cast is celebrating at the summit with the Final Curtain waiting to be drawn across a Menai sunset.

Instead, there is a sharp twist. Cathy decides not only to walk away from Christopher but also climbing and her climbing friends to return to Tooley Street. Here, out of a sense of duty, she intends to marry a feckless former boyfriend who has spent the duration of the novel in Borstal. Longland found it 'unsatisfactory artistically' and Perrin was sufficiently outraged to rewrite the ending as a ghost story. The latter's disbelief is understandable as he must have seen a number of parallels between Cathy and himself, not least in the attitude of the 'Everesters' to the emerging city hordes.

But being annoyed by the ending is one thing, suggesting a realistic alternative is another. Cathy could have become a professional mountaineer. Gwen Moffat showed that it was just about possible for an unattached woman to succeed in that sphere and Longland's introduction to her autobiography, *Space Below My Feet*, could be read as an apologia for Cathy if she had chosen that option. Putting aside the disparity in family support—Moffat's mother was at hand to bail out when necessary—it would nevertheless have been nigh on impossible, short of *One*

Green Bottle 2, to persuade the reader of the day that such a scheme was realistic.

The Dramatist's alternative solution could have been a suitably heroic death accompanied by whatever passes in mountaineering circles for flights of angels. This would have been quite easy to organise and could have the usual tragic range from hubris—a solo attempt on Suicide Wall—to self-sacrifice—in the act of saving one of Bootle's little urchins. But such a course would inevitably be melodramatic and the great strength of the novel is that it avoids those excesses which Holland so successfully ridiculed.

In fact, it could be argued that the conclusion is artistically consistent with the rest of the novel. There is no suggestion that Bill or Tooley Street has been ultimately rejected. The former is revisited at regular moments in the novel and it is clear that because Bill is out of sight, he is not also out of mind. The fact that she justifies sleeping with Leonard Head by convincing herself that she did it for the boots rings the uncomfortable bell of Bill's pitiful excuse for stealing: 'Cathy! I did it for you.' And there is more than a suggestion that she believed that the moment in question properly belonged to him.

There is always a feeling that Cae Capel is an

interlude, never a final destination. Cathy finds it hard to believe that a hill she can see from Craig yr Isfa could possibly be the same one she could see from the Wirral. Red lights bob as the bicyclists from the hostel slip down the pass to catch the last train. Walkers hitch a lift home on a lorry. The imagery tugs in one direction.

Perhaps what was really unsatisfactory for Longland was that Cathy got less than he felt she deserved. He probably believed that social mobility through opportunity was the key to future happiness. In retrospect, we can see the downside of this worthy scheme. The Establishment plundered the quality that lay in the working classes and used it for its own ends. But the other part of the equation is too often ignored. If all the strength were to go, the rump would have neither inspiration nor support. Longland and Perrin might not like it, but they cannot, to suit their own purposes, remove from the novel its case for feminine altruism. In the end, Cathy is one green bottle that doesn't accidentally fall.

It could be that the better genre than the novel is that of the short story. It has the greater artistic opportunity to imitate the subject matter. The classical unities of time, place and action can be observed and combine as the piece's individual energising force, and there is a potential connection between a rock climb and the structure of a short story. A good example of this is 'The Vertical Ladder' by William Sansom. It is a climbing story but not in the true mountaineering sense.

A young lad sets out to impress one of the girls in his group. Even though he has a morbid fear of heights, he accepts a dare to climb to the top of a gasometer. There are two ways to the top: a fire-escape set of stairs and a Jacob's ladder clamped vertically to the side. The dare is to climb up the vertical rungs rather than the easy stairway. The bottom section of the former has broken away but access to the missing fifteen feet is made possible by a ladder they 'borrowed' from some absent workmen. The boy reaches the bottom rungs and begins to climb. His plan is to stare steadfastly in front and move up one step, one foot, at a time. However, the sound of laughter makes him glance down. The cause of the amusement is that the ladder has been removed and any possibility of retreat cut off, and the group is starting to drift away in search of other entertainment.

His only choice is to continue. So, afraid to look

either up or down, he closes his eyes and lifts a hand to clamp on to the next rung before making any further upward step. Thus, with always three points of contact, he edges towards safety. Eventually, he senses rather than sees that he must be near the top and continues with a growing sense of confidence. He reaches up again but cannot locate the rung. He opens his eyes. The last few feet of the ladder have rusted through and broken away.

Although this is not a mountain story, its construction owes much to the drama of any enthralling mountain tale. First there is the crossing of a Rubicon—the Eiger story would lose a good deal without the Hinterstoisser Traverse—to be followed by the moment when, unable to retreat, it appears impossible to continue. 'The Only Blasphemy' by John Long, anthologised in *Mirror in the Cliffs*, exploits this situation to the full and captures in prose all that is involved, both physically and mentally, in top-grade climbing. A lower-key account of similar circumstances is found in C E Montague's 'In Hanging Garden Gully', although in this case the impasse is more the result of miscalculation through over-caution than misjudgment of the technical challenge.

There has to be some outcome, actual or left to the reader's imagination, but the usual denouement that results in the waving of the triumphal ice axe can have a different twist, as it doubly does in the Montague story. The literary endgame can be as interesting as any other that climbers play and 'Last Climb' by Martyn Berry, unpublished until it was included in Wilfred Noyce's *The Climber's Fireside Book*, makes full use of this opportunity. Two young men have completed their first climb on Cloggy and walk to the summit to watch the mushroom cloud rise slowly above Liverpool.

Climbing is also used as an adornment in a variety of other prose genres. The ghost story is well served by presumed deceased climbers appearing (or disappearing) through the mists of time and various Ben Macduis. But it was Showell Styles, under the *nom de plume* of Glyn Carr, who put his mountain knowledge to the most effective literary use. The corpus is a series of whodunits set in and around the various mountain centres of the author's acquaintance. Although there are excursions to the Alps and Norway, the best, in the sense of the most convincing, are set in Snowdonia. Like Coxhead, he is able to use familiar topography and well-known rock climbs for his own purposes. Usually it is to prove the possibility, or otherwise, of someone being, in mountaineering terms, in a certain place at a certain time. To this he adds the spice of technical detail to entrap those villains who cannot tell their bowline from their granny. Moreover, the choice of North Wales can only help the maker of mysteries, having as it does a backdrop of diabolical kitchens, furtively suspicious natives and routes redolent with macabre nomenclature.

His choice of detective, Sir Abercrombie 'Filthy' Lewker, Shakespearean actor-manager of the old school, sets the tone as he filters through his cast of suspects, which usually includes: nice young girl, pushy, not so young, girl, maddish professor, obligatory bounder, and lantern-jawed chap gripping pipe and rock face with equal determination. These are supported by the usual red herrings in the form of Alpine Guides, disreputable hippies and Boy Scouts. Nevertheless, like Sir Ab, the stories rattle along with a certain brio and there can't be many publishers who would produce fourteen sequels to *Death on Milestone Buttress* unless they were pretty sure of an enthusiastic market.

An interesting and different extension is the

historical novel or a type of docu-fiction. A recent example is *Hazard's Way* by Roger Hubank, where fictional characters mix with real members of the past. Much of the action is set in Wastdale Head at the hinge of the nineteenth and twentieth centuries, thus allowing a variety of climbing enthusiasts to populate the novel. Some, such as Collie, Oppenheimer and the notorious Aleister Crowley, are real whilst others, who make up a mixed bag of schoolmasters, doctors and academics, are fictitious. Hubank took advantage of what turned out to be an unofficial moratorium on the exploration of new and harder routes. The Old Guard felt that the risks taken by the likes of O G Jones had been unjustifiable and that the existence of such routes was bringing their pastime into disrepute. The untimely death of Jones on the Dent Blanche seemed to prove their point and for a decade the Fell & Rockers (as they were to become), rather than push up standards were happy to repeat the routes of their Victorian forebears.

This circumstance offered the author a literary advantage. It allowed him to present, without any historical inconsistency, his fictional characters Lockhart and Widdop as the leading young climbers of their generation. They could repeat the difficult routes of the day and, given the restrictions, avoid new ground—any attempt on the Great Flake of Central Buttress, for example, would have been incongruous to say the least—without raising critical eyebrows. Yet their historical presence allowed the climbing folklore of the time—billiard fives, the stable door traverse and the legendary exploits of OGJ—to be fitted seamlessly into the text.

The protagonist, a reluctant medical student, sees Wasdale as a bolthole from his filial duties and his activities there mirror the main plot, which is entwined within the rights and wrongs of the Boer War as an act of colonial oppression. Eventually fiction and reality collide. First, a game of Scouts and Outposts, a mountain-based version of Hide and Seek, points up the theme of appearance and reality that has previously described Britain at war. Then a party of four led by Lockhart, who has become obsessed with the possibility, attempt a direct ascent of Scafell Pinnacle from Lord's Rake to Hopkinson's Cairn and perish in the attempt, in exactly the same manner as did the real life Henry Jupp, A E W Garrett, R W Broadwick and Stanley Ridsdale in the renowned fatal accident of 1903.

Whether the genre could be developed is open

to question. No doubt the doings at Pen-y-Pass and Sligachan could provide sufficient local colour to fit the bill and a suitable plot could be woven around the exploits of Winthrop Young and Mallory, or Maylard and Solly, with the Abraham Bros filling in the cracks. But it is hard to see it emerging beyond the sepia-tinted mists of that era. Whillans, Brown and the Creagh Dhu could provide the folklore but the biographers have had a large bite and it would be difficult to imagine recent hard men as peripheral figures in a plot controlled by more ambitious individuals.

Any account of mountain fiction would be incomplete without reference to *One Step in the Clouds*, compiled by Audrey Salkeld and Rosie Smith. This omnibus of mountaineering novels and short stories has an erudite introduction which should sharpen the appetite of any enthusiast. It is wider-ranging than a review of British storytellers. It includes American writers, prose drama and more recent developments of the twentieth century. Not surprisingly, there is a section on aspiring women. But whether it is a good idea to isolate the female contribution, as if it were a genre of its own, is a matter of debate, as much in mountaineering as in literary circles.

The Comedy of Humours

In a pastime where failure can mean being 'dropped' in a rather more permanent manner than being sidelined to the Reserves, it is not surprising that climbing's associated humour tends towards the gallows variety. Much of this is anecdotal and a fair proportion springs from the doings of the less conservative elements of the mountaineering world. Tales similar to that of the solo climber finding his earnest request for a rope answered by a neatly coiled version landing on his head are not untypical.

My own experience in this field was amongst the limestone tors of Dovedale. In those days limestone seemed to be generally exempt from the golden rule, handed reverentially down from one generation to another, that 'the man who would drive a piton into British rock is the sort of man who would shoot a fox'. Routes that in due course turned out to be Just Medium Very Difficult if sprinkled with liberal doses of the appropriate calcareous powder, generally bristled, at the time, with various pieces of ironmongery.

A chance meeting with a salesman of life insurance had persuaded me to purchase one of his policies. The sales pitch was that, out of the commission earned, he could buy and we could share the necessary hardware to attempt a projected assault on the soaring cliffs of the Dolomites. This seemed like a reasonable idea at the time, probably because the only dolomitic limestone I had thus far encountered was that of Rainster Rocks near Brassington, whose soaring cliffs, though admittedly steep, struggled to rise above the tree line. Moreover, the general ravages of time had produced holds that were literally jug handles or would serve as thread-belays to hold the hawser of a decent sized ocean-going liner. If this was dolomite climbing, it seemed all right to me.

Nevertheless, we thought it best to sharpen our claws on the aforementioned outcrop before attaching ourselves in a semi-permanent manner to the Cima Grande. So we cadged a lift to Dovedale with the local climbing club and set off for the sharp end of mountaineering. This decision had the added bonus of advice dispensed by a man on the bus, who seemed to know his bongs from his skyhooks. 'If I were you, lads, I'd start on Cave and Arête. Once you're on the overhang, it's a quick pull and jugs all the way to the top. Give you a good idea of the standard.'

We followed his directions and found ourselves in the cave. It was straightforward enough to climb the back wall until the roof was reached. This had convenient cracks in the various leaves of rock that formed its ceiling, which in turn offered secure pegging to its lip. A suitable combination of tension and étriers allowed the exit point to be reached with relative ease. Peering round the bulge, I was delighted to see a peg *in situ* within arm's reach. Clip in, pull up on tension and good holds were for the having. There were even a number of cracks that appeared to have been especially designed for the drilled-out hexagonals that had been the previous zenith of our machine-tooled sophistication.

Whilst 'easing over the crux', a phrase I had always associated with the effortless movement of feline grace and power, two events occurred, seemingly simultaneously. The first was that I found myself hanging upside down a few inches from the floor of the cave, the second was my companion banging his head on its roof. This was accompanied by the sound of uncontrolled laughter as our mentor and his acolytes fell out of the surrounding undergrowth. The peg on which I had balanced the weight of my ambition was of a variety known as an Ace of Spades which had been loosely placed, doubtless on their last visit, in a suitably narrow horizontal crack. As its name suggests, it is sufficiently broad to take a downward pull in such a situation but lacks the mechanical construction to withstand an outward tug. As long as the rope was under tension, all was well. Once the tension was released, as the climber moved upwards and outwards, it sprang out as readily as a rotten tooth.

Disconsolately, we unravelled the *mélange* of our misfortune and slunk off to try something that appeared in the official guidebook. Eventually this involved turning Ilam Rock into a Derbyshire *via ferrata* but, at least, a summit was reached. Though, it seemed, at a price. Despite all attempts on both ascent and descent, there remained the inevitable, unremovable piton. Rather than leave a key piece of our equipment, I had an idea. If we attached the peg to one of the ropes we could, once on terra firma, take advantage of the fact that the pinnacle was situated on the floor of a valley. By climbing up the bank we were able reach a point level with the object of our desire and using our combined strength rip it from its resting place. After a mighty struggle there was movement and the piton, now alloy dart, guided by the catapult effect of extended nylon, fizzed through the air to embed itself in the trunk of a tree just above our heads. It was probably at this point that the purveyor of life insurance realised that he had a greater responsibility to his Prudential employers than to his newfound companion and our ambition to form a climbing partnership to rival the titans of the past came to a speedy end.

Virtually all biographies or expedition accounts have similar embellishments and these, for the most part, seem to be the limit of humour in climbing literature. The more sustained effort is difficult to find. A renowned exception is *Ascent of Rum Doodle* by W E Bowman. This description of the attempt on a 40,000 foot giant discovered by Allied airmen overflying Yogistan during the Second World War is rightly acclaimed for its efforts in debunking the myth of mountaineer as hero. However, although there are useful insights into the London Transport System and the psyche of the Alpine Club, Bowman's main concerns lie outside the domain of a book that deals with mountaineering in Britain.

Notwithstanding, there is a scattering of home-grown examples where the humour is central rather than peripheral to the piece. These are most often in the form of the sardonic or satirical essay that starts life in a climbing journal or magazine. A typical example of this is 'Welsh Rarebits' by Baldwin Shaw, published in the 1939 Climbers' Club Journal. As the title suggests, it is a medley which deals with the difficulties occasionally found by the uninitiated. 'The Tryfaen Gully Game' has long been held as an absolute proof of the adage that it is better to travel hopefully than to arrive. Tom Patey was probably the master of this genre, although C F Holland's 'Rupert' essays and Menlove Edwards' forays into the psychological undergrowth are part of a longer, if more gentle, tradition.

The comic short story turns up occasionally and Graham Sutton's 'The Man Who Broke the Needle' was rightly included in Fell & Rock Journal No 70 that celebrated 100 years of Lakeland rock climbing. But the best collection is exemplified by the writings of G J F Dutton in his series of tales of the Doctor and his friends and their exploits in *The Ridiculous*

Mountains. These tales started life, for the most part, as separate accounts in the Scottish Mountaineering Club Journal but were later gathered together and published by Diadem Books in 1984. The format of each is broadly the same. Three companions set off on a venture of their own design, only to arrive at the outcome via a variety of unexpected deviations. It is a common enough literary strategy and the skill depends on the author finding the right blend of characters to produce the desired effect. The poles are held by the vertically advantaged Doctor, who represents all that is old school, and the Apprentice, who is all layback and state-of-the-art gear. The middle ground is occupied by the narrator, who vacillates between the two in an attempt to gain a position of moral, emotional and especially physical security. This is a useful authorial device as both parties of the extreme assume the third man to be of their camp and consequently take him into their respective confidence. As a result, Dutton, posing as narrator, can observe and colour his history to taste.

The usual ongoing debate surrounds the ideal nature of the proposed outing–the Doctor preferring a mouldering heap of rock and heather held together by crumbling ice and snow, preferably preceded by a five-mile hike through a midge-ridden glen, with the Apprentice leaning towards a more stable substance somewhat nearer creature comforts. Inevitably, the Doctor, with the sole means of transport, gets the upper hand, leaving the Apprentice to salvage whatever he can. The surprising thing is that the Apprentice bothers at all, instead of following the more obvious course of climbing with his fellow 'Weasels'. Eventually the reader realises that there are certain advantages to be had, should any potential bird-in-hand heave over the horizon, in avoiding the competition of his peer group.

The gist of most tales is the attempts of the others to modify the Doctor's ill-considered ambition. Nevertheless, the outcome usually deals the Doctor the last laugh as he is for the most part impervious to failure or quick to assume that any turn of Fate's wheel is the result of his own rotation. A good example of this is the aptly named 'Chalking It Up'. The story revolves around a long-standing discussion of the ethical use of climbing equipment, the relative efficacy of tricounis over plimsolls, etc, the debate usually ending with a homily along the lines that you can always shorten the length of a long-handled axe but never achieve the mathematically opposite effect. This left, at best, an Apprentice Parthian shot that the Doctor's trusty length of five-millimetre line could always come in handy for tying up any stray parcels they might stumble across.

However, in this particular story, the argument takes a correlative turn. The Doctor, who had chanced across some Hard Men's Mags showing 'waves of golden Apollos swarming effortlessly up the impossible', declared that as climbing had returned to its proper state, i.e. unfettered with such artificial aids as ropes, he would be willing to join his companions in their attempt on Constipation, a new HVS on the Ben. Later sobriety cast doubts in some minds on the wisdom of the decision but the Doctor was not to be deterred and, sporting the now *de rigueur* chalk bag, he joined his friends on the hill. The Apprentice's anxiety had extended to his bringing all measure of ropes to ensure, if not the best possible solution, at least the best solution possible to the inevitable catastrophe and he and the narrator spent the walk to the cliff explaining the use and value of the red rope, the green rope, the fixed rope, the free rope, etc, etc, with no apparent evidence that the message had got through.

Eventually the inevitable happened and during a necessary short pendulum, the Doctor not only swung wildly off route but also on to the holdless crux of the ferociously artificial Purgative, and in his efforts to free the now inextricable tangle of ropes managed to detach himself from their support altogether. His antics were watched by both his companions anxiously, and with interest by a gang of English who felt earlier indignities might now be compensated for by the forthcoming entertainment. The Doctor, by placing his hand in the chalk bag, then patting the rock, moved inch by inch up the slab until he reached a small ledge where a rope could be re-attached and he could be reeled in. *Ecce Homo!* The first man to complete Purgative without aid. Later explanation reveals that the 'chalk' was not chalk at all, but strategically placed limpets. This, as the Doctor explained, was not really using aid in the strict sense of the word. In fact, nothing could be more traditional. As they were alive, the success was due to use of the combined tactics so favoured by his heroes of the Golden Age.

The indignity that the anticipatory English had suffered was at the hands of the rightful occupants of their illegally invaded Hut. This re-enactment of the Battle of Bannockburn had ended in a similar outcome. In fact, much of the pleasure of the stories comes from such asides, which take a swipe at a variety of institutions. Munro-baggers get their fair share of scorn. Not only is the ascent of the Reverend Zoar McKinley McSigh's final Munro accompanied by a bevy of Compleat Munroists, each bearing his or her own number in the table of ascension, looking for all the world like 'sufferers out of Dante', but Geordie and Wull, stalwarts of the Pittemdoom Cairn Gatherers, are forced to make a variety of cameo appearances. Their distrust of steepish rock or snow lying above the horizontal is explored in 'Fixing Us Up' (another tell-tale title) and 'A Wet Day'.

Nor are the protagonists themselves immune from ridicule. The Doctor, in one of his seventy-four inch pontifications, decides that as they are climbing in the Highlands all communication on the rock face should be in the Gaelic, with the not unexpected disastrous results, and the Apprentice's attempt to impress his latest female appendage with a hirsute appendage of his own quickly comes to grief in subzero temperatures. The stories also keep pace with their times and mingle sea-stack climbing, outdoor centres and the military, not to mention a feisty American lady who, having torn the appropriate diagram out of the Apprentice's 'not inexpensive' guidebook, solos into the ether over the nearest overhang.

The writings of Tom Patey, although overlapping and indeed simultaneously appearing in the SMC Journal with Dutton's stories, are of a darker tinge. His tone is both sardonic and satirical but it is the sardonic that appears to have better survived the test of time. His account of the televised attempt on the Old Man of Hoy, which concentrates for the most part on the climbing, with an occasional acerbic aside, seems to me to work better than when, in 'The Greatest Show on Earth', another sea cliff television foray, he deliberately adopts a more satirical voice.

The opening of the former describes Patey trying to persuade a fellow passenger that their intended attempt on the tottering pinnacle now lying off the starboard bow and being systematically destroyed by the Pentland Firth, was a legitimate target for his party's ambitions. His audience was sceptical. Apparently even the Army had failed and 'they' had used rockets. Patey played his ace card, explaining that his two companions over there (Bonington and Baillie) were no less than recent conquistadores of the Eigerwand.

'You mean,' enquired his audience, gesticulating

towards the side rail, 'the two gentlemen who are being sick?'

This seems, to me, to be essentially funnier than 'The TV Armchair Guide to Mountaineering' with its 'Snap Link—a Link that Snaps' variety.

Patey's humour, and perhaps all humour surrounding climbing, seems to work best when observing the antics of others; none more so than in 'A Short Walk with Whillans', an attempt on the Eiger, where his companion's 'proverbial bluntness' is put to good effect. Apart from the title, which as a piece of controlled understatement could hardly be bettered, the thumbnail sketch of Whillans as man and climber is subtly woven into the piece to produce a picture a lesser writer might well labour over. This is more successful than the caricatures that populate, say, 'The Professionals' which are often little more than thinly veiled references to figures in contemporary circles, as in the circuit lecturer, 'Crispin Bonafide'. The trouble with this sort of writing is that it relies on the reader understanding the in-joke, which rather undermines any attempt at serious satire. Like the office memo, which can often be a cheap shot, it requires a firsthand knowledge that by definition is denied to readers of a later generation.

Using the individual to represent the general can be done, as Pope and Dryden showed. I am not sure that Patey, although he would have been at home among the Augustans, has quite the poise or, more probably, the ambition to reach those heights. His likely aim was just to entertain a perceived audience and to that extent it works well. His series of chancers in 'The Art of Climbing Down Gracefully', with their variety of ploys to avoid putting their money anywhere near their mouths, is neatly drawn but lacks real sting and relies unnecessarily on existing prejudices (for example, all Oxbridge types are 'handicapped' by their common background) for comic effect. Even 'Apes or Ballerinas?' which with its revealing epigraph from Darwin and arresting opening sentence promises much, tends to degenerate into a swipe at the over-sartorial Continental who swans around the catwalks of sun-kissed granite.

This assessment has one serious flaw and that is that it assumes the label of satire attached to one portion of *One Man's Mountains* meant Patey had the serious intention of wishing to reform by holding folly up to ridicule. The collection was put together after his death and the various sections may be no more than an editor's attempt to put some form and order into a number of disparate pieces, rather than any claim by the author himself. In fact, the more you read the more you realise that his humour lies not in sneering at others but in an understanding of himself. Selective self-deprecation usually works well, as the subtext to his photograph in *The Commando* under the caption 'Men Who Dare' clearly shows.

I was interested to find when initially researching material for various chapters that pieces that relied on humour for their success were for the most part written by Scotsmen. It may be that the form gives the ideal opportunity to have a go at 'The English', a term which, in some circles, does not so much relate to the inhabitants of that nation as act as a catch-all expression to cover all forms of perceived wrongdoing, regardless of perpetrator. There again, it is possible that Scottish climbers have more time on their hands waiting for climbs to come into condition and, tiring of the crossword, have turned the mind to higher flights.

Or perhaps the Celts have a greater sense of the ways that language can be used. This is certainly true of the Welshman, Selwyn Russell Jones. His comic climbing verse was first published in *Climber and Rambler* and examples are to be found in Walt

Unsworth's anthology of mountain humour, *This Climbing Game*. The wit is essentially epigrammatic. It exploits the dark potential puns thrown up by climbing references such as 'deadman' and 'the cornice too had a curling lip'. But comic verse must engage the ear as much as the mind and, at their best, Jones' lines have a vigour and tautness that do. In 'Mission Aborted', a fool's errand of a rescue, the Land Rover has just slid off the edge of the road where 'Sid hit the ditch in a skid'.

> *For a ditch is all right on a warm summer's night*
> *For a kiss with a miss who is blissfully tight*
> *But a ditch is a bitch when you pitch off the track*
> *Into four feet of slush with the wheels sliding back.*

But regardless of race, examples of climbing humour seem to be relatively thin on the ground. For the majority of categories of writing, I found I was usually spoilt for choice. In fact, I could be easily persuaded that I should have chosen better texts as illustrative matter. I am not sure why this gap exists. Perhaps, it indicates a serious inadequacy in my reading. Perhaps after all, climbing, even if it is taken over-seriously at times, is still a serious business and being too flippant, too often, could well be tempting fate.

Location, Location, Location

Any body of writing that relates to mountaineering must contain examples of authors who have a real sense of place. The literature of British mountaineering is well served in this respect. Perhaps particularly so, as the relatively small scale of the hills in this country encourages a sense of intimacy. This, in turn, prompts the reader to explore for him or herself and, in so doing, dovetail the mutual experience of imagined circumstance with that of reality on the ground. For, unlike most other sports, there is a real connection between stadium and sportsman. Sometimes it is the sweep of the solitary view that conjures the prose to match the subject, as in Neil Munro's description of Rannoch Moor in *The New Road*:

Its nearer parts were green with boggy grass, on which the cannoch tuft—the cotton sedge—was strewn like flakes of snow; distantly its view was sombre—grey like ashes, blackened here and there with holes of

> *peat. The end of it was lost in mist from which there*
> *jutted, like a skerry of the sea, Schiehallion.*

At other moments there is a tight compression, the hill under the microscope, if not the knife, as in Archer Thomson's renowned description of the penultimate pitch on the 'Exceedingly difficult and delectable' Great Gully of Craig yr Isfa:

> *The cave is spanned by two huge boulders forming bridges. The further is the easier of access. By utilising a small foothold on the right wall the climber effects a lodgment upon it, and then reaches its sharp upper edge by a struggle, in which he comes near to defying all the laws of anatomy. A novel expedient is to lay the palm of the right hand on the block, and using the arm as a pivot, perform a pirouette to the south; the climber thus lands in a sitting position, with one leg thrust upwards to the roof to maintain the equilibrium ... Any Gallio, however, will complacently demand a shoulder.*

Traditionally, the principal climbing areas of Britain have been located in three places: the Highlands of Scotland, the Lake District and North Wales. Each has its own atmosphere and devotees, both on the crags and on the page. Good mountaineering literature contains more than descriptions of striding triumphantly to the summit or clinging defiantly to various bits of verticality. The better writers manage to convey the sense of being among the hills, the sense that you are in hill country. It is hard to put your finger on when hill country begins and it happens before you are overtaken by towering peaks and tumbling streams. I used to travel regularly from the north east of England to climb in the Lake District. I can't remember exactly where, but there was a point on the journey when I felt I was about to arrive. Rock started to outcrop from the now lighter coloured grass–Lilliputian Gable Ridges and Scafell Pinnacles. Regardless of what might have happened during the week before, I felt a surge of excited enthusiasm and the foot pressed harder on the accelerator.

Starting from the top, there can be no author who has shown a more complete understanding of the hills of the Highlands and Islands than Bill Murray. Multi-striking Munroists may have visited more tops more often and individuals may have visited more outflung outposts or clung to greater perpendicularity, but their range of experience is usually limited. Murray examines the anatomy of his chosen country from the bowels of Clachaig Gully via the Cioch of the Cuillin to Arran's Rosa Pinnacle. Not that the author is dependent on looming cliffs or glittering ice towers to catch the flavour. A chapter in *Undiscovered Scotland* describing a mountainous stravaig where the day's total ascent and descent could not have been more than a couple of hundred feet, gives perhaps more the feeling of the Highland landscape than any other.

'The Moor of Rannoch' describes a double crossing of this particularly lonely piece of land. The summer of 1949 had been gloriously hot and Murray reasoned that the terrain should be as dry as it ever would be. Indeed, apart from river crossings and regular bathing in the lochs, he managed the journey with dry feet. The route was from a point between Loch na Stainge and Loch Ba to Rannoch Station, then back to the Kingshouse via Black Corries Lodge. A reading of the chapter gives a compendium of much that confronts the hillwalker in the Highlands.

First there is the size: fifty-six square miles of relative desolation. Murray saw neither deer, hare nor grouse, despite the best efforts of his dog to raise whatever game there was, and no humans at any time. Such was the solitary state that he quickly realised the unnecessity of re-dressing after each of the many plunges into the bays of Lochs Ba and Laidon. It is a huge bowl of a moor, circumvallated on all sides except for a single loophole that allows the accumulated waters to flow via the River Tay into the North Sea. Its expanse allows a new perspective, and mountains, foreshortened when approached close to, suddenly attain their true proportions.

Then there is the land. As Murray rightly says, in this sort of country distance is 'measured in time not miles'. A river crossing had to be abandoned at more than one point as the water rising to the chin threatened to upend him and the rucksack balanced precariously on his head. In all, a half-mile detour was necessary before a reasonable crossing could be effected. There was little in the way of easy going and even when an 'excellent track' was found marching in exactly the right direction, it petered out into a sheeptrod after a few hundred yards. As always on the second half of a Highland journey, the heather grasped more tenaciously and the folds of the land became more time-consuming. Of habitation there was little. A railway station in the middle of nowhere, a ruined cottage called Tigh na Crua-iche and the deserted Black Corries Lodge.

The chapter concludes with a question. Had the effort been worthwhile? Moors, like mountains, don't come easily, at least the best ones don't and this is the particular mark of the Highlands. But with the going getting easier and the thought of a good meal at the Kingshouse, the response was already forming. He had seen the moor in summer. But what about in winter, when the low-lying sun would skim off the frozen lochs and a solitary ice-bound tree would become a 'flashing chandelier'? Out of the question if the snow was soft but if, frozen hard, it had filled the dips, bridged the rivers and turned the heather into a surface resembling tarmac, then 'all should be more than well'.

And it is the likelihood of just such conditions that separates the Scottish hills from those in more temperate climes. For not only can they offer delightful walking but they also convert even the most modest ascent into a different challenge. As Murray points out in the chapter entitled 'Tournament on Ice', the fact that a man has done a rock climb in winter means nothing unless you know exactly the nature of the conditions. Summer difficulties can disappear under a bank of snow and a simple scramble in June can become a tentative February dance on fragile ice.

In other words, any route undertaken in true winter conditions is effectively a first ascent. The route the chapter describes is the first winter ascent of Shelf Route on Crowberry Ridge. In summer, it is graded Difficult and its 550 feet would take little over an hour for an average party. When Murray and Mackenzie completed their ascent it was a ribbon of continuous ice and took the best part of a March day.

Winter conditions can additionally have other causes for concern. In Scotland they are more Arctic than Alpine and one January Murray, with his companion Mortimer, decided on a traverse of Liathach that included a preliminary ascent of the North Pinnacles Route. Their estimate was eight hours. In fact it was thirteen hours later when they eventually reclaimed their tent from the elements. The problem was not so much the technical difficulties as mist, gale-force gusts with driving snow, sleet and eventually rain. They climbed between squalls, sheltering as best they could when the worst of them arrived. One of the most ferocious beat Mortimer in the race and swept him off his holds. Fortunately they had decided to rope up for this section.

Once on the ridge, route-finding was reduced to guesswork for nothing could be seen 'through the veils of snow and hail'. They struggled over the summit and stumbled down into Coire na Caime, a topographical feature only identified when they pitched knee-deep into the snow-covered lochan. At last they reached their tent, left sopping clothes outside and dived into dry sweaters and sleeping bags to hear 'the music of a ... primus' and watch 'pure snow turn in the pot to grey slush, then to bubbling clarity'.

The chapters cited are to be found in *Undiscovered Scotland*, published in 1951 as a companion volume to the better known *Mountaineering in Scotland*, written by Murray during his internment as a prisoner of war in Italy. The latter, part of his battle to keep some sense of perspective, deals in the main with the more popular climbing areas of Glencoe, Ben Nevis and Skye. *Undiscovered Scotland*, as its name suggests, goes further afield, not only geographically, and examines the effect that mountaineering has on man. It is, to my mind, a better picture of the Highlands—a place where you have to travel hopefully, yet be prepared to struggle before finding the blessed relief, if not of mystic enlightenment, at least of dry socks.

Harry Griffin's descriptions of Lakeland had a very different genesis. His first book *Inside the Real*

Lakeland grew out of the countryside notes produced for *The Manchester Guardian* and these in turn grew out of his early boyhood and adolescent experiences. He lived as a child in the south-west corner of the Lakes, when Furness was still part of Lancashire and that county's highest point was Coniston Old Man. His first hill was Black Combe, the highest point visible from home. Still in short trousers, he privately considered the ascent quite an achievement, even if it wasn't something to brag about. And that attitude underlies much of what he wrote. He is more proud of his beloved fells, crags and tarns than anything he might have achieved amongst them and the homage shows through. *Inside the Real Lakeland* captures the flavour of the region as a whole and his descriptions range from the Sports at Grasmere to mutton and rum butter. But despite this attempt at an overview, the fells and rock climbs are always at the margin, itching to get in.

So his second book *In Mountain Lakeland* is, as its title suggests, about the real 'Real' thing. First, there is a section on the fells themselves. Coniston Old Man is a firm favourite, not only for its omnipresence in his early exploration but also because it is a modest peak that does not 'lord it over his vassals'.

It has, moreover, been generally beaten up by a variety of excavators in search of mineral wealth but has remained unperturbed by the indignities. It is therefore not surprising that Scafell is preferred to the vertically superior Pike. Not only are its rock faces steeped in the greater history and lichen, but its summit plateau, uniquely, affords views of its fellow hills in Scotland, Ireland and Wales. Myth has it that the north-facing cliffs of Craig yr Isfa were first discovered from Scafell by a man with, we might assume, a rather large telescope.

Although his list includes the usual suspects, Helvellyn and the Langdale Pikes, it is also more selective than those that cater for the centrally-based tourist. He is equally enthusiastic about the then often neglected northern fells, that stretch of land known as Back o' Skiddaw. Even today, with a decent start, you can have considerable chunks of the place to yourself and are able to explore the delightful Mosedale and surrounding fells with little more than solitary curlew for company. Of all these hills, Carrock Fell is the most interesting. It seems to have got lost. Its crags are Skye-like gabbro and the heathers are more Scottish than Cumbrian. It is a geological jumble where Skiddaw slate has collided with a variety of volcanic eruptions. The result is a wealth of mineral deposits including, it is said, uranium.

But the substance of the book is about the rock climbs and those who climb them. 'The Pioneers' is a chapter that traces the history of the sport and 'Steep Places' gives an interesting and accurate account of the climbing in the district. Griffin's timing was fortunate. At the time of writing, development in the Lakes lagged behind the exploits of the likes of the Rock and Ice in the Peak District and North Wales. The Central Buttress of Scafell was still the premier route it had been four decades before, so his account seemed not only accurate but also complete.

Nevertheless, times were in the process of change and although, understandably, he is more at home with the climbs and climbers of his own generation, he is quick to praise the skill and tenacity of climbers such as Paul Ross and Pete Greenwood, who were putting up hard new climbs in and around the Borrowdale area. A different type of writer of the day might have found it easy to sneer at their penchant for crags that did not involve a day's march on the hill or dismiss their routes as unnecessarily artificial variants of the great routes of yesteryear. Griffin saw them as yet another added laurel.

Climbing in Cumbria seems more embedded in the community than elsewhere. Jim Birkett, whose post-war climbs with their sustained steepness upped the standard in the district, made a living in his playground. Griffin recalls Birkett's pride on seeing Cumbrian slate used as a key feature in the rebuilt Coventry Cathedral. Bob Graham, who set a record walk over forty-two peaks within twenty-four hours, was proprietor of a Keswick guesthouse. Alfred Wainwright, whose guides have done more to popularise Lakeland hillwalking than all the rest put together, was Kendal's Borough Treasurer. Griffin knew it is the people as well as the topography that make the place and his writing reflects their contribution.

Water, by definition, is integral to the Lake District and hill or cliff reflected on its surface is a favourite composition for artist and photographer. Griffin reminds us that the district is made up of more than the obvious Ullswater and Windermere. There are nearly 500 tarns of various shapes and sizes for the explorer to come upon, each imprisoned in its rock and turfy setting. Yet another local, Timothy Tyson, bathed, albeit briefly, in each and every one of them. This was not a stunt, as Griffin explains, but part of an attempt to understand the district as a whole. Therein lies the place's charm. You can, if you want to, really get to know the Lakes. Unlike the Highlands with its hundreds of separate peaks, where even the most determined traveller merely scrapes the surface, the Lakeland hills are relatively few and abound with paths, so, as Wainwright proved, all their various ways can be covered well within a lifetime of weekend outings.

And what this means for someone like Griffin is that he is able to dwell on the detail. His observation of the flora and fauna is never a dull catalogue. Whether he is describing the aerial acrobatics of the raven or distinguishing the two more common varieties of alpine campion as 'fadder dees' and 'mudder dees' (if you pick the red one your father dies, the white one your mother) you catch the vitality of a man caught up in his own enthusiasm. More books followed, turning over more stones, rooting out further nooks and crannies. Perhaps his greatest gift is to make you realise that despite the tourist industry there are still many places where you can have the place to yourself or with those you choose to be with. As Jack Longland put it in his foreword, he 'genuinely communicates enjoyment of uncomplicated pleasures'.

If you searched for something to describe the dominant feature of North Wales, I feel it would be cliffs and, if pushed for a colour, you would probably choose black. So it is logical to assume that the Soper/Wilson/Crew account of the doings on Clogwyn du'r Arddu is a not inappropriate choice to represent the region. The volume charts the history of climbing on Cloggy from the historic beginnings in 1798 to the book's publication in 1971. If my previous writers have relied on their own experience to recapture the favourite parts of their own country, it took, not for the first time, combined tactics to sort out *The Black Cliff.*

In the early sixties, Rodney Wilson decided to collect as much information as he could find and piece together a history of the cliff. Unfortunately, his efforts were so thorough that the material got out of hand and publishers, though interested in the idea, thought the nature of the project rendered it 'impracticable and uneconomic'. Peter Crew, aided and abetted by Ken Wilson, took an interest and persuaded Jack Soper to rewrite the manuscript. In 1970 they found a publisher.

The format is a series of chronologically ordered chapters that chart the exploration of the cliff in its various stages. Each chapter is preceded by an apposite epigraph that summarises the current state of play and is fully illustrated with the appropriate photographs. This latter contribution by Ken Wilson is an essential complement to the text. Because much of the information is drawn from journal articles written by the perpetrators of the new routes, the description of the difficulties and the position they found themselves in is often understated. The juxtaposition of Crew's account of the first ascent of the Great Wall and Wilson's succession of pictures is a good case in point. In addition, Cloggy is a complex cliff for the uninitiated, who would have found it difficult to envisage the whole without some form of visual aid, and the number of people who were intimately familiar with the topography in 1970 would hardly have added up to a print run.

The book contains a full index and a short bibliography. It would, however, have been useful to have more detail of the 'many articles and references to the cliff in club journals'. It is to be assumed that Rodney Wilson unearthed more than appears on the page and it would be interesting to discover what ended on the cutting room floor. What does work well is an alphabetical list of pen-portraits of climbers who have contributed to the history as it unfurled. Interleafed is a series of thirty-two portrait photographs, ranging from Abraham to Yates, which is effectively a Hall of Fame for those who have done so much for climbing in North Wales.

Inevitably, as you look through the names, you wonder who made the greatest contribution. Where in the relative order of things do Longland's, Great Slab, Vember, Great Wall stand? If it is a question of breaking a psychological barrier, a rock-climbing equivalent to the four-minute mile, they could all have a shout. No route of any consequence had been completed on the main part of the cliff until Pigott and Longland put up their eponymous climbs. Others must have looked but retreated, convinced of George Abraham's dictum that 'the easy places are too easy and the difficult places are impossible'. To have opened the gates of Arddu, as the book puts it, was no mean task when every step was into the unknown. When Kirkus climbed the Great Slab, the step was a stretch longer. With no runners he launched himself into the middle of a 600-foot expanse of virgin rock with no hope of assistance if matters went awry. Brown's determination on Vember, despite a previous long fall and the knowledge that it had defeated Kirkus, together with his host of other new routes, could bear the palm if it were not for Crew's single-mindedness to outmaster the Master.

But Cloggy is used to controversy. The debate over artificial aid has, like the mist, continually hovered over the cliff. I suppose it all started in 1798, when Peter Williams hauled his fellow Reverend up the difficult bits of the East Terrace with the judicious use of his belt. The reportage of the ascent of Pigott's seems to be as much concerned with the insertion of Morley Wood's (in)famous pebbles as it does with climbing. Over the years there was a range of acrobatics in the form of human pyramids and when, on one occasion, these combined tactics failed to achieve the graspable target, it was suggested that the lightest member of the party should be hurled upwards in search of the holds. There were leaps by Linnell, tension traverses and a variety of alarming pendulums. As the authors point out, it is to be wondered what these good old boys would have got up to if they had been given access to karabiners.

Some of these antics were not always intended. In 1948 'Scottie' Dwyer and Dick Morsley attempted a long-awaited second ascent of Edwards' Bow-Shaped Slab. Faced, if he fell, with a long pendulum off the first pitch, Morsley declined to follow. Dwyer declined to return. 'So they took their separate ways to the top, Dwyer up Bow, Morsley up Great, connected by 200 feet of hemp line and belaying each other as best they could.' As time went on, the points of aid and controversy increased and, appropriately, *The Black Cliff* closes with a debate on the ethics of ironmongery. At what point do you distinguish between the use of an inserted pebble, a nut, a peg, or a bolt? To what extent does the argument change when the offending items are used for protection rather than aid? And, given the compact nature of British climbing, does the use of external assistance negate the very point of doing it?

The whole book reads like a thriller. In fact, in one review, the Banner/Crew guide to the crag was advertised as more gripping than the latest James Bond. Whether this was due to the laconic style, the use of state-of-art gadgetry or the Machiavellian tactics employed in the early sixties is not clear, but there is no doubt that, when they looked between the lines, a number of readers were considerably more shaken than stirred. The cliff deserved its reputation. As the early explorers quickly discovered, there were no obvious lines of graduated difficulty so that they could feel their way on to the cliff. No 'New West' splitting the West Buttress which could provide a possible escape route or vantage point from which to assess other difficulties.

To step off the ground meant you believed you were a VS climber and until 1959 when, as Whillans so succinctly put it, 'Everybody will be doing them when the sun comes out', on-sight VS leaders were still thin on the ground. What is as relevant is that, like Scafell, Cloggy's position at around the 3,000-foot contour offered a number of excuses for spending the day on more low-lying crags. At every point in its development it had taken a group of particularly determined individuals to make the next step and *The Black Cliff* is a fitting tribute to their endeavours.

What these books have in common is that they were concerned with describing unfamiliar territory. Much of Scotland at the time of writing was certainly 'unknown'. The Lakeland described is a real version, not the tourist variety packaged round Dove Cottage and orange peel on Scafell Pike. And in the 1960s you didn't have to queue for many routes on Cloggy.

There is, however, when the deifying pen is poised, always the danger of the hills being too much alive with the music of worship or heroic struggle. It might therefore be appropriate to point readers towards a passage from Giusto Gervasutti's inspirational autobiography *Gervasutti's Climbs.** He was climbing alone in the Dolomites and had reached a point where his progress was blocked by a chockstone, the lip of which overhung into space. He pulled up on its edge, only to find that it was too rounded and protruding to allow sufficient purchase for the necessary mantelshelf move. He then discovered, on lowering his body, that he could not locate the footholds he had pushed up from. A second attempt was equally unsuccessful. His strength was failing and the 1,000-foot void loomed. Fingers slipping forced a final effort which, using every part of his available anatomy, including chin and teeth, left him shaking and exhausted above the obstacle. He recalled his immediate feelings after the adrenalin levels had subsided. The valley below him lay peaceful, the rock on which he had just struggled, indifferent. He realised that it was he alone who had caused the moment. This was no adversarial conflict, just a man pushing his luck.

*English translation (by Nea Morin and Janet Adam Smith) published by Rupert Hart-Davis in 1957 and reprinted in 1978 by Diadem Books, now administered by Bâton Wicks.

A Scot or Three

 In the 1960s I took up a teaching post in Cheshire and, among the usual paraphernalia that announces the start of a new academic year, was ceremoniously handed a register of my future pastoral charges. Given the geography, I was somewhat surprised to find on it so many names of obvious Scottish origin. But there they were, the MacIntyres, MacDonalds and MacGregors jostling for position with the more indigenous Mannions, Moores and Mottersheads, whilst the aboriginal Brocklehursts, Baileys and Bracegirdles peered down on the offcomers as their forebears must, in times of social change, have peered before. Nor was my class list unique. Scattered throughout the school were a variety of Celtic outposts caused by ICI's decision to close its Scottish workplace and shift the attendant force to Macclesfield.

Inevitably, a portion of the adult males found its way around the local hostelries and amongst this particular diaspora there are two who linger in the memory. Although both had their origins in the east end of Glasgow, they seemed to occupy the extremes of intellectual sensibility when dealing with their enforced exodus. Hughie, particularly as the evening wore on, took it upon himself to defend the honour of Clydeside as an area of outstanding beauty by describing at length, if not always in depth, the vista from his auntie's window spreading crimson towards the westering hills. Ernie also had views but for the most part they were on the precise nature of the English, whom he regarded on the whole as rather dull-witted.

His chief delight was to lead his victims through a maze of logical contortions until at last they fell exhausted into the carefully prepared trap. As a teacher of English, I was a prime target.

'Now here's one for those scholars of your English boys' grammar school' (said in such a way as to establish the immediate supremacy of Celtic wit and the Scottish educational system). 'Do you think they could write down correctly to my dictation a simple sentence?'

I wait, mouth closed.

'It is a very simple sentence, the sort of sentence

that even an Elementary boy could manage, yet I'll buy you a dram if you can produce me one of your' (a deliberate search for the appropriate term) 'chaps who can do it.' (A hiatus whilst the landlord produces pen and paper.) 'The sentence is: *There are three ways of spelling'* (a slight pause) '*the word...*' At this point, a rather longer pause before, with the slightest of smiles, he uttered that particular monosyllable of sound which in the English language can simultaneously mean the numerical adjective between one and three, the preposition indicating motion towards and an adverb denoting additional degree.

Several decades later I read the biography of the Scottish mountaineer, writer and broadcaster Jock Nimlin, written by Ian Thomson, and as the pages turned I heard the same combined echo of sentiment and savvy that I'd first heard so many years before. Nimlin was born in 1908, so his early adult life was spent in the material and spiritual deprivation that was then the lot of much of the British working class. Clydesiders could do little about the collapsing economic world which denied them the opportunity to work for a living, but they could take certain matters into their own hands. Groups of mostly young males would leave the grime and misery of the city and escape into the open air of the surrounding hills. A favourite venue was rural Milngavie and a wooded hollow beside Craigallion Loch, where fires would be lit, tea brewed in communal gallon cans and songs composed and sung. In fact, the Craig-allion Fire seemed to burn continuously, for many of the unemployed decided to spend at least the summer months in the wooded shelter, leaving it only once a week to collect the dole. Their numbers were swelled by the weekenders and soon the Fire became a symbolic gathering-ground for protest and socialist hope. Thomson entitled Nimlin's biography *May The Fire Be Always Lit*, a key line from the Craigallion Fire Chant.

Some were happy to remain in the surrounds of Milngavie, but there were others who were more restless spirits and explored first the Lomond area, then, like ripples in a pool, further and further afield. Nimlin was such a man and he recalls the lengths to which he and his companions would go to reach the cliffs of Arrochar and Glencoe. If fortunate enough to be in full-time employment, they would be unable to leave Glasgow until Saturday evening, yet have to be back at work by Monday morning. So any form of transport was more than acceptable, ranging, in

Nimlin's case, from a hearse to a wagon containing a tethered but still interested bull.

There was, of course, no money for overnight accommodation and an art was perfected in constructing howffs out of natural rock formation, augmented by any locally available material. There were also a number of shelters offering tempting alternatives that the landowners had erected for their own self-indulgent purposes. From time to time, to thwart the perceived invasion of their property, the said landowners would triumphantly raze the buildings to the ground, only for their remnants to arise as an ingenious construct, often christened with suitable irony. The proprietorial behaviour was, however, in stark contrast to the attitude of those who actually worked on the land. Wherever he went, Nimlin befriended crofters and shepherds who would put him up and share their food. In return, Nimlin would run messages from the city for tobacco and the like.

It was around the Craigallion Fire that the Ptarmigan Club was founded by Nimlin, as was the more renowned Creagh Dhu by Andy Sanders. Both were formed specifically for working-class climbers as a response to the Scottish mountaineering scene.

The only two existing clubs that had any standing were the Scottish Mountaineering Club and the Cairngorm Club. Membership of both was eminently middle-class and, because of the carnage of the First World War, decidedly elderly. Such a concoction would not have appealed to Jock Nimlin. An alternative combination of fellow workers would not only provide comradeship—indeed at times the *esprit de corps* verged on the tribal—but also the opportunity to pool resources to support their various needs. In particular, there were the co-operatively hired buses. The most renowned of these, 'The Mountaineer', was owned and driven by Charlie 'Flee-on' McAteer, who did not consider the odd snowdrift or two a good reason for abandoning the journey. On one occasion, the passengers had to disembark and clear the road from Crianlarich to Luss, a distance of twenty-five miles, before meeting up with the result of municipal-driven snowploughing.

I am sure Thomson would be the first to acknowledge that the strength of his book lies in his direct quotation from Nimlin's own writings. Unlike the members of the established climbing clubs with their bulletins and journals, Nimlin had no natural outlet for his efforts and, instead, had to compete in the commercial world of professional journalism. In 1950 he wrote an article for *The Glasgow Herald* that recalled an early experience of witnessing 'a father of Scottish mountaineering' performing a perfect standing glissade 'with a gleam in his eye, a flush on his cheek and a thick powdering of snow crystals in his beard'. Nimlin was clearly attracted by this exhibition of apparently effortless control and it became an ambition to emulate such a faultless performance. When reading the piece, you quickly realise that a similar ambition must have lain behind the balance and purpose in his prose.

Suitably, his better described ventures are after the SMC-ites had scuttled back to their hotels, leaving him to savour the hills from his various outdoor eyries. The accounts of a night at the Shelter Stone–the highest bedroom in Britain–and New Year spent at the Observatory on Ben Nevis capture the moments denied to those ruled by the gong that summons them to, if not Heaven or Hell, at least various unmovable feasts. On the Nevis occasion he was delighted to be treated to a 360-degree view of the Highlands and Islands in which the snow-covered hills of the Cuillin, Kintail and Cairngorm were merely the middle ground.

Although, like the individual himself, his writings range across the mountain experience from rescuing less than grateful sheep to a winter retrieval of two ounces of tobacco abandoned by a divinity student on the summit of Ben Macdui, he also produced more orthodox reports about newly completed rock climbs. His party made the first ascent of Raven's Gully on the Buchaille in 1937 and he was the first man to climb the crux pitch in Clachaig Gully in the same year. He had to abandon the climb at this point as the bus was about to leave and Bill Murray, unaware of Nimlin's effort, completed the first ascent the following year.

Perhaps the piece that tells most about the man and the true nature of climbing in Scotland at the time is his description of a winter ascent with Bob Peel of Tower Ridge on the north face of Ben Nevis. This eventually appeared in an article for *The Glasgow Herald* fourteen years after the event. To the modern reader, the most striking part is the inadequacy of the climbing equipment, a point that had already been illustrated in an account of a climb on Bidean nam Bian, where Nimlin had ordered his second to exchange boots so that he could have the crucial advantage of the better nailed footwear. In this case, on the Ben, his ice axe was too long to be of much use on the critical pitches and eventually became so much of a hindrance that it had to be abandoned in favour of literally clawing his way through the snow and ice until his fingers and a couple of nails found some scrapes of rock on which he could take 'a strenuous rest'.

Such was the continuous strain on the muscles involved that when they reached the horizontal section that connects the ridge to the parent mountain and started to walk, the change of use resulted in a violent attack of cramp in the thighs. The outcome, Nimlin recollects, was that he was reduced to 'sliding along on one knee and trailing a rigid leg'. Once the summit plateau and comparative safety were reached, the 'long accumulated tension disappeared like a wisp of snowdrift', to be replaced by the oxymoronic dull elation that so often follows the conclusion of a momentous physical struggle. But they made no attempt to sort out the conflicting emotions that swept over them. 'It was sufficient that the moon was shining ... across the hills and glens, and, if anything clouded our minds, it was no more than the thought of starting a well-frozen Austin into life again.'

On certain issues he was more forthright than effusive. By and large he, like many before him, disapproved of guidebooks. He believed that the essential point of mountaineering was exploration rather than the dogged following of others' footsteps, even to the extent of replacing the piece of turf that had concealed the key hold on his Very Severe finish to the Cobbler's Right-angled Gully. And he was in no way equivocal when it came to the use of pitons. In an article for the SMC Journal in 1958 he stated that any use of artificial aid was unacceptable as it implied that the perpetrator assumed that the limit of free climbing had been reached. Clearly this had never been the case in the past and was unlikely to become so in the future. As he aptly put it, with more than a hint of his family's Rechabite views, 'some climbers came to possess pitons and ... it wasn't long before the pitons possessed *them*'.

Ironically, the war returned relative prosperity to Clydeside. Nimlin acquired a job as a crane driver with Harland and Wolff where, 150 feet above the shipyard, he no doubt had as good a view as Hughie's aunt. He also, in moments of inactivity, had time to compose his articles and broadcasts for the BBC. On Sunday 31st January 1943 a programme appeared on the Home Service under the title 'A Shipyard Worker Speaks'. In it Nimlin argued that the fight against Fascism was not limited to the overthrow of Germany but also of the inherent Fascism of the existing social structure in Britain. His ideal for the future lay around good housing, good education and a right to work. The Attlee government implemented much of what he proposed but sadly ignored his suggestion for future housing which meant 'a system which would help the occupier to become the owner whenever he has paid the house value in rent'. If this had been adopted, then much of the current greed, fuelled by expectation of (in)equitable plenty, might well have been avoided.

As for the hillside gathering, it was extinguished by the war. Once peace returned, an attempt was made to resurrect the mood and the call went out for The Boys to meet in a Glasgow tavern. The old songs were sung with the old fervour but everyone agreed it was not the same. So a symbolic one-off reconstruction was staged. But the new landowner had alerted the police, who arrested the leaders (i.e. those with the warmest seats) and soon after that the loch was drained. With it died the embers, though perhaps not the spirit of the Craigallion Fire.

Always a Little Further, written by Alastair Borth-wick, was published in 1939 and similarly describes the weekly exodus from Glasgow for the great out-doors. Indeed, with its reference to the Howff of a Thousand Draughts and camp-fire singing, it would appear at first sight to cover the same ground and many of the dramatis personae contained in Nimlin's biography. In fact, the great man appears as early as page 17. However, Borthwick and his companions come from what he describes as a sheltered upbring-ing and it was more chance than intent that brought him into contact with the likes of the Ptarmigan and Creagh Dhu.

As preparation for a planned camping holiday on Skye, Borthwick and John Boyd decided to spend a weekend at Arrochar. Dismayed at the crowds resembling Sunday in a Glasgow park, with its attend-ant domestic disturbance, they decided to climb a nearby hillside and pitch their tent high above the turmoil. It was a measure of their inexperience that they believed that in all probability no human being could have camped there before, and they discussed the forthcoming holiday and their plans for some low level walking. But to them, as to Brutus, between the acting of the thing and their first motion came, if not a phantasma, at least the arrival of an equally startling 'Hamish'. In fact, his name was not Hamish at all (and one can only assume that whatever forename his parents deemed proper was insufficient for his purpose of enthusing all at hand as to the glories of ascending vertical rock). Such was his zeal that within twenty-four hours he had not only persuaded the pair to take up climbing (for their Shangri-La was beneath the rock faces of the Cobbler) but also to change their Skye plans to include, exclusively, the Cuillin.

So Borthwick's life-compass swung in a violently new direction and after the Skye escapade, which involved a two-and-a half-day walk-in to Glen Brittle without eating, climbing down the West Ridge of the Inaccessible Pinnacle by mistake and a near fatal disaster on Sgurr Mhic Connich, he duly discovered the dubious pleasures of Dan Mackay's barn, long distance hitch-hiking and agreeing to Hamish's often harebrained schemes. But his curiosity led him into a nether world beyond the working-class clubs formed by Nimlin and Sanders. A world of flatties, minks and haakers, the tramps and tinkers who would gather for the berry-picking at Blairgowrie and in turn initiate the author into the dangers of insulting a female mink or accepting a Dundee Sandwich. And in this process of discovery, which involved spending a night in a wagon with a dead sheep resting on his companion's shoulder 'like a dyspeptic lawyer' and assimilating Choochter's advice on how to succeed in the surreptitious arts of competitive hitch-hiking, where the scriptural pronouncement that the last shall be first finds no better evidence of proof, he realised that what he had to tell was 'not a novel or a biography' but 'a collection of short stories, each with its own characters'.

As a result, we are presented with a mixture of anecdote both personal and historic, coupled with a photographer's eye for colour and form. This concoction of drawing pictures and telling tales lies at the heart of his success, no more so than in his account, following 'a night of black and silver', of a twenty-five mile crossing of Rannoch Moor. More orthodox mountaineering accounts interleaf but their central thrust is less the technical nature of the climbing, more a detached appraisal of a particular moment of interest. These could be threatening—nearly being harpooned by an ice axe in the Upper Couloir of Stob Ghabhair—or, in the case of the dangers of overeating before descending the more constricted portions of Am Basteir, instructive. The final piece, 'The Chasm', a description of the then hardest climb in Glencoe, deserves to be in any climbing anthology. It is a brilliant composition of humour and suspense, culminating in a denouement that has the protagonists balancing precariously on the very edges of tragedy and farce.

As for his philosophy as to why he climbs, it is simple: to escape a modern world with its 'multitude of petty worries'. Or, as he put it, 'One cannot sweat and worry simultaneously.'

On 31st January 1980, four members of the Outdoor Education Diploma course from Irene Mabel Marsh College, three students and their instructor, were swept into the sea while traversing the zawns of Anglesey's South Stack. The students were saved. The instructor, John Cunningham, the foremost Scottish climber of his generation, who couldn't swim, was drowned.

This is a synopsis of the prologue to Jeff Connor's biography of Cunningham but, as the title *Creagh Dhu Climber* suggests, the book is as much about probably the most notorious climbing club this country has ever produced as probably its most renowned member. Although formed at the same time and under the same circumstances as the Ptarmigan and Lomond Clubs, it attracted a particular membership whose reputation for intoxicated violence was not entirely unmerited. Although many of the stories that surrounded their doings were inevitably apocryphal, they were a breed apart who were quite prepared to sail pretty close to the wind. Membership was by invitation only and required 100 per cent consensus, which was not readily given. For those interested in the ongoing saga of events at Jacksonville, the true story of the battle of Zermatt and the interaction of climbing and industrial Glasgow life in the years around the Second World War, *Creagh Dhu Climber* has plenty to say on the 'Bonnie Fechters'.

Nevertheless, if any man could claim to be *the* Creagh Dhu Climber, it has to be John Cunningham, and the main thrust of the book is devoted to establishing this claim. After the war, numbers dwindled and the Creagh Dhu looked as though it was going the same way as the Craigallion Fire, though one suspects with more of a bang than a whimper. However, the Club President, when beginning to accept the inevitable, noticed two young climbers on the Cobbler. Rather than follow the time-honoured practice of working their way through the grades, they instead followed Lyon and his presidential party around the cliff, completing route for route. The newcomers were Cunningham and his climbing partner Bill Smith. Lyon realised that if the likes of these could be persuaded to join the Creagh Dhu, the club might be revived.

Cunningham did more than this. With routes like Gallows Route (E1) and Carnivore (E3) he changed the face of Scottish rock climbing and brought the standard up to the speed that was beginning to emerge south of the border. More importantly, he used his new-found authority to insist that all new members had to be serious climbers, even to the extent of blackballing his own brother. The result was that Cunningham and Smith were not isolated shooting stars but merely the A team that headed up a clutch of fine climbers like Patsy Walsh and Mick Noon who were able to climb at a similar standard in their own right.

Unsurprisingly, these efforts did not meet with universal approval. Their attitude was regarded by the Establishment, and even senior members of the Creagh Dhu, as cavalier and their tactics dubious. Cunningham eventually gave up sending accounts of new routes to the SMC as it would reject them on such spurious grounds as choice of name. Much of this disapproval must have bordered on jealousy. Because the new climbs were uniformly graded, at the most, Very Severe, though now recognised as covering the ground from Mild VS to E4, it meant that the pre-war classics were inevitably downgraded and many of the established and long-valued views challenged.

The Scottish mountaineering establishment was not the only target. The Creagh Dhu also despised chancers of any sort, particularly Englishmen with a high opinion of their own ability. Any such were directed to a 'wee little problem you might find interesting', which usually turned out to be an epic struggle on the Direct Finish to a waterlogged Raven's Gully while the Creagh Dhu stole and ate their food. Although he was less parochial than the traditional Scottish mountaineer and was prepared to learn from the advances being made in England and Wales, Cunningham was no exception to those who delighted in putting down the English. His advice was, on one occasion, sought on the nature of placements on a difficult-to-protect E2. Asked what gear he had taken when he did it, he replied a number four hexagon. The leader failed to find a crack that would take the hexagon or, for that matter, anything else and sustained a long and quite serious fall. On recovery he confronted his adviser.

'I thought you said you took a number four hex?'

'Aye, that's what I took.'

'But I couldn't find anywhere to place it.'

'Funny that,' replied Cunningham, *'neither could I.'*

I have a feeling that Ernie would probably have approved.

Shafts of Light

As has been mentioned in an earlier chapter, mountaineering literature began to take shape in the form of articles written by members of the Alpine Club. However, it is unlikely that these authors would have thought to claim the loftier title of 'essay' for their work. To do so would suggest that their efforts attempted to follow the venerable footsteps of Addison, Hazlitt and Locke and so had, by implication, something of consequence to say on the human condition. Such a claim would have been at odds with general opinion. Clambering around hills was all right for the rude peasant in pursuit of the elusive chamois or errant sheep, but no activity for a gentleman. To believe otherwise would be to fly in the face of such luminaries as Shakespeare, to whom 'mountaineers' were deformed human life, exemplified by Caliban in *The Tempest*, or Queen Victoria, who suggested the activity should be proclaimed illegal after the disaster on the Matterhorn.

So, in a climate that assumed that mountain climbing belonged somewhere between the lunatic asylum and the Indian rope trick, it is understandable that its exponents did not wish to flaunt their folly too openly.

Unless, of course, they could find an acceptable reason. And to the Victorians nothing was more laudatory than the advancement of science. If, unlike patriotism, it is not necessarily the last refuge of a scoundrel, it has from the cure-all 'sholder boon' of Chaucer's Pardoner to the current application of Heath and Safety regulations been at times a cloak for the real purpose. So, if they could demonstrate by the ascent of an appropriate aiguille the true nature of atmospheric pressure or, by sharing mutual rocky fissures, discover the existence of a hitherto unknown member of the arachnid family, it was surely perfectly acceptable to describe, en route, how these observations came to light.

Even after the pretence had been dropped, the format was not and an apologetic tone was *de rigueur*. As a result, much of the writing is tainted by false modesty or motivated by a desire not to break ranks. At best it is anodyne and therefore of little interest to the reader. At worst, in an attempt to hold the party line, it induces a confusion of thought. I was always bemused that a generation which deplored the use of pitons and saw such artificial aids as another example of the triumphalist Fascist jackboot being ground into the face of humanity should openly applaud those who used oxygen to invade the holy places of another culture.

When *Hill-writings of J H Doughty* was published, there was no question of modesty, real or otherwise, on the part of the author. The decision by H M Kelly and the Rucksack Club 'to bring together under one cover his essays on mountaineering' was intended as a tribute and memorial to a member who, despite his early death, had contributed so much to the club in particular and mountaineering in general. The claims made in the introduction that Doughty's writing has 'humour, wisdom, breadth of outlook and clarity of thought' does not overstate the case and to appreciate this variety the collection should be read as a whole as the subjects swing to and fro. They vary in colour and form, yet are always seen through the same very individual prism.

Not many, for example, would choose an ascent of Lingmell as the *locus classicus* to illustrate the attraction of Lakeland mountaineering. Most would require the crutch of respectability offered by the choice of Pillar Rock or the Central Buttress of Scafell. Even Eustace Thomas, who had visited most corners of the fells in his successful attempt to complete 30,000 feet of ascent in one journey, could not find time to visit this modest outlier of the Scafell massif. The Lingmell occasion, as often the best of occasions are, was the result of chance or, rather, a chance remark. On an earlier expedition Kelly, the then leading exponent of Lake District climbing, had just completed the Girdle Traverse and, questioned as to what the party should tackle next, replied, 'Let's do Scafell. I've never ticked it off.' Whereupon the party, somewhat bemused, 'solemnly followed him to the summit cairn'. So when a similar question was posed after a hard session of step construction in the depths of Skew Ghyll and Cust's Gully, the proposal that they should 'go on to Lingmell' seemed not entirely inappropriate.

In fact, Doughty seems to have an eye for the peripheral. In 'Nomenclature' he takes an interest in the various names that have been given to Lakeland climbs from the beginning of such registry to 1933. As a schoolmaster who taught mathematics, it was not long before he had put them into subsets which he catalogued as Personal, Alphabetical/Numerical, Topographical and Descriptive. The last grouping was something of a catch-all, including as it did those of the imaginative, cryptic and miscellaneous variety. As he explains, Type 1 was not quite as vainglorious as it seems. Slingsby's Chimney and Jones's Route were shorthand for a more long-winded explanation belonging to a small group who 'passed the butter round pretty industriously'. But the modern climber is left with the question as to who were Pavey Ark's Gwynne and Scafell's Professor after whom chimneys are respectively named.

He felt that the middle two types had serious limitations. The Alphabetical/Numerical lacked imagination and the Topographical, after you had squeezed the Nor'-Nor'-West between the North-West and North climbs, ran the danger of 'boxing the compass'. Perhaps he did not know, or chose to ignore, that the naming of Routes I and II on Pillar reflected less the 'arid, unimaginative and benighted' inventive powers of the perpetrators than the stuffiness of senior committee members who objected to the forthright and possibly more accurate suggestion of Sodom and Gomorrah, which would clearly belong to Type 4.

It was just such names that caught Doughty's interest. He wonders whether the first ascent of Toreador Gully involved a 'desperate encounter with a savage bull' and ponders 'what curses first rent Blasphemy Crack, what orgies initiated the Cocktail Route'. He is more than happy that the name should be founded on a joke but feels it should be shared rather than private. He gives, by example, the route on Ravenstones christened Wedgewood Crack. It was not born from 'one whose love for the applied arts was stronger than his spelling' but, as the guidebook explains, 'summarises instructions given during the first ascent'. The Wood in question was Morley, who had a turn of mind of which Doughty clearly approved. After completing a new route on Castle Naze, Wood decided on the name Pilgrim's Progress, for not only did it finish at Paradise Corner but, as with Huckleberry Finn, he had found it 'interesting, but steep'.

Doughty goes further. Not only should the joke be explained but also approved. To that end he suggested 'the institution of a climbing-naming committee of the Fell and Rock Club' and even offered, free from copyright, a list of possibilities for the future. He felt it unlikely that he would use any for himself but, if they were taken up by later generations, he saw it as an 'interesting inversion of the natural order of events' which might 'add a spice of interest to [his] declining years'. The last on Doughty's list was Hobson's Choice, and indeed a route on East Wall of Pavey Ark climbed by J W Cook and A R Dolphin some thirteen years later now bears that name. Sadly, it was a decade too late for it to serve its purpose.

One advantage of having an author's work collected by others rather than chosen by him/herself is that the outcome can often include pieces that the originator might well have regarded as too insubstantial. Kelly concludes the volume with 'A Group of Reviews' and 'Extracts From Editorials'. Doughty's assessment of the writings of others is generous but in no way sycophantic. He suspects that much of Winthrop Young's reputation has been built on indiscriminate hero-worship but is quick to acknowledge *On High Hills* as a masterful example of the ability to entwine the threads of doing, seeing and feeling. With others there is shorter shrift. G D Abraham's *Modern Mountaineering*, in Doughty's opinion, isn't and the reviewer feels that 'a writer must bring more to his task than a limited tolerance and a trailing of ancient glories if he is to appeal to the younger generation', though the book is otherwise 'eminently readable'. R L G Irving's *The Romance of Mountaineering* suffers a more obvious damnation through faint praise. After questioning the author's wisdom in overflaunting the 'old school tie' and indulging in 'silly gibes at Communists', he concludes, 'These are superficial blemishes ... To those who share his views on social and mountaineering questions his book should prove an unalloyed delight.'

There is the inevitable touch of the pedagogue about him. 'An agreeable picture of a familiar scene' for those 'not disposed to worry over the final niceties of syntax' appears as much a swipe at perceived falling standards in general as at F S Smythe and his particular *Alpine Journey*. But the harangue is never without humour and has a greater aim. Much anticipates Orwell's political essays and novels. Both men saw the dishonesty that can be disguised by language. Orwell's writings may have occupied a greater canvas but, in his capacity as editor of the Rucksack Club Journal, Doughty set about the task of encouraging his contributors to examine the way they wrote. Among those matters that troubled him was the use of the passive voice: 'The hut was left at midnight and the foot of the rocks reached three hours later; here a halt was made for breakfast.' He felt this produced 'an excessively strained effect' and at worst was little more than a cloak for false modesty.

His real 'foul fiend', however, was what he termed 'the inverted comma disease, an insidious malady that seems to be on the increase'. First, he despised the use of the device to perform the function of spoken inflection or bodily gesture as 'nebulous and capricious'. But the more objectionable was its use to excuse slang or sloppy expression. He saw the likes of *We set off to 'bag' another peak* as a 'shabby gentility of letters, the written correlative of a self-conscious giggle'. Orwell, of course, takes the whole matter much further, feeling that the corruption of language is instrumental in the corruption of thought and that politicians deliberately abuse meaning to justify the unjustifiable. Doughty is not nearly so forthright but he did broach the subject nearly twenty years before the author of *Nineteen Eighty-Four*.

Indeed, I am sure that the man who, as a boy, chose to be a Labour candidate in the school's echo of the 1906 General Election would have had an affinity not only with the greatest socialist writer in the English language but also with a man whose essays, according to *Geographical Magazine*, are 'as fine as anything that has been written about climbing'. Jim Perrin deserves this accolade. His writing ranges over the whole mountain scene, which is observed with good humour, compassion and, at times, understandable indignation. His first collection, published in 1986, is called *On and Off the Rocks* and opens with a section entitled 'The Gilded Calamity'.

This, for the most part, is about the people and hills of North Wales. Perrin has written about many parts of Britain but there is always a feeling that Wales is his spiritual mountain home. His essay 'Where the Need Exists: A Reverie' describes when 'the spell was first cast', how he met a welcoming Welsh couple who imparted a sense of place and culture that was to remain with him in all that he wrote. In fact, the landscape and the people both past and present merge in his mind and form an amalgam that holds his ideas together. 'A Small, Gothic Cathedral of a Mountain' crystallises the method. In it he describes Tryfan and the routes to its top in the way you might an old friend whom we will, of necessity, eventually part from, 'each into his darkening valley'.

It is clear from a reading of the essays in this

section that Perrin values wild and solitary walking but, like Doughty before him, he is soon drawn into the argument as to whether the hills are for the benefit of the (self-identifying) discerning few or for the many, regardless of how they might behave. In 'Men, Women and Mountains' Doughty quotes Sir Claude Schuster who, whilst feeling that his Alpine tour had been spoiled by the rising popularity of weekend skiing, where 'huts are hideous within with a noisy joviality and without with empty tins and other ghastly reminders of the activities of man', is forced to admit that 'It is churlish to deny this right. Indeed one cannot but regret that similar opportunities are not open to the aspiring youths of these islands.'

Fifty years later Perrin looks at similar problems in North Wales. Unlike other high lands in Scotland and England (a trip to Wasdale is never a light undertaking) those of Wales are easily accessible to the surrounding centres of population in the West Midlands and South Lancashire. The hollows are conveniently placed to collect the rain driven by the prevailing wind and the constructions at Rheidol, Stwlan, Trawsfynydd and Dinorwig with their 'footpaths, car parks, toilets and restaurants' have replaced the previously impoverished 'rough, rocky stretch of water flowing into a tiny gorge under a very utilitarian bridge'. The heights are continuously kicked into submission by a multi-millipede of boots that in a decade can cause more erosion than a millennium of rain and frost. 'A Sacrificial Mountain?' enters the political debate to weigh the pros and cons of this circular conundrum—people erode footpaths, conservancy agencies restore with artificial roads, thus encouraging more people to erode more paths. It all leaves the writer a little nonplussed.

When it comes to *On* (as opposed to *off*) *the Rocks*, there is a different lodestone and the stone is grit. Ever since he first scrambled on Windgather Rocks in the course of an early excursion from Lyme Park to Lud's Church, the short but steep escarpments that litter the southern Pennines have held Perrin's imagination. So it is no surprise that the first two pieces that concentrate on rock climbing are centred around the problems that this particular rock formation throws up. Natural as opposed to quarried gritstone climbs have a basic plan. They are either slabs seamed with horizontal faults or steeper walls split by vertical cracks. The former require a good sense of balance, the latter the ability to hand- and toe-jam. The essay 'In Praise of Jamming' is a celebration of this particular technique and explains how the mystery was revealed to the author at Helsby Crag. Reading it, I recalled a similar visit to the gritstone of Gardoms Edge. The absence of the sort of handholds I had previously experienced at the given grade was rather disturbing and the day's itinerary planned in the glow of the previous evening's alcoholic hubris was subject to a rapid revision. However, like any piece of legerdemain, explanation tends to spoil the effect. As a friend of mine put it when describing Goliath's Groove on Stanage: 'There's really nothing to it. You simply start at the bottom and ratchet your way to the top. Quite straightforward really.'

And 'straightforward' is the proper epithet. Most gritstone climbs are 'simple' but it is wise not to confuse that term with 'easy'. Perrin's second essay in the section is 'Right Unconquerable: a Gritstone Paean'. This route on Stanage was long admired and first climbed by Joe Brown in 1947. To Perrin it is, like Cenotaph Corner, a keynote climb, more a test of attitude than technique. There are no cunning passages or contrived corridors for an old man to hide in: '... the way is sealed by the base of a jutting flake. Above lie step on step of overhanging flake, thirty feet and the crux at the top … If you do the climb at all, you do it quickly.' With Right Unconquerable, as with many gritstone climbs, what you see is what you get. But you also get the impression from Perrin's writing that there is more to gritstone than a springboard for advancing standards on greater cliffs. Not far under the surface is a social comment. As the Victorian Alpinists looked askance at those who were content to concentrate on the cliffs of Pillar Rock and Scafell's northern face, so did the latter, for the most part middle-class professionals and academics, in turn look down on outcrop climbing. Perrin, brought up in a now flattened part of Hulme, is proud of the achievements of his antecedents and is pleased to cherish them.

There are, of course, other climbs in other places, often lovingly described—none more so than the Ogwen Valley in 'The Land that Time Forgot'—but I feel that it is not irrelevant that, when reading from his biography of Don Whillans at the 2005 Leeds International Festival of Mountaineering Literature, he chose as his illustrative passage not some epic on a Himalayan or Andean giant but a description of Chew Valley and its attendant Wimberry Rocks. It was here that Perrin, as Whillans a decade before him, had discovered the pleasures of wild walking and climbing on what the 1965 guidebook described as 'a very fierce crag'. The chosen passage comes from the chapter that closes the book and acts as a coda to the life of Whillans. Greenfield can be reached by a bus from the centre of Manchester and Chew Piece by a walk along 'the dye-stained beck that flowed down past the mills' before the patch of green is reached where tents can be pitched. It was a progress made not just by a couple of individuals but a couple of generations, separated by a world war, who wanted to escape 'the stockade' of industrial conformity.

Perrin remembers such escapes in 'Trains, Cafes, Conversations', a piece in the fourth section that examines the reasons that lie behind climbing, and in the third, 'The Human Factor', recalls the people who for one reason or another caught his imagination. On the surface, H W Tilman and Al Harris are unlikely bedfellows but the essays point up the connection and show how they both belong to the group who 'have had an influence on the way [he thinks about or looks at] aspects of the mountain experience'. His interview with Chris Bonington is particularly revealing, showing depth to a character that is easily caricatured. But in all these probings there is a sense that the author is searching for himself as much as those he writes about, a desire to find his own position in the scheme of things, to distance himself from and yet be part of what he will eventually term 'Life in the Climbing Village'.

For me, if this is the dynamic that gives his essays their strength, then it is the range of his prose that provides the agility. A grammar school education effected a collision with Milton which in turn shunted him into Blake, Housman and Hardy. He stretches for these literary co-relatives when he writes, not as a display of gratuitous erudition but as hooks on which to hang and display the textured pattern that discovery has woven. His prose is always on the move. He can pass from people to places, from thought to feeling, from the profane to the sublime without offence to either party. Yet he can sit still and watch others move. Still enough to recognise that a primus does not purr but 'growls', or observe 'the moon showing through gaps in the cloud brilliantly edging the fretwork of trees'.

The second selection of essays, *Yes, to Dance*, follows a similar pattern and is a development of and sequel to *On and Off the Rocks*. In many ways it is more assured, at times more polemic, and the early lyricism, though still there, is somewhat muted. Themes previously explored are revisited, none more so than in 'Green Pieces' where the author's feelings about the desecration of wild land by a variety of agencies fill him with rage. The problem is analysed in 'The Death of Reverence and the Birth of Despair: Reflections on the British Mountain Scene'. This was written in 1986 and was an important part of the protest that was growing at the Government taking over tracts of land for 'essential military purposes' and consequently preventing their use for recreational activities. Even when his case is strongest, Perrin is also aware that the story has two sides and questions the degree of responsibility shown by climbers in their use of the environment. In 'Trespassers' he surreptitiously records the views of the owner of Craig y Forwyn who was attempting to prevent climbers from using the crag. On hearing the full story, his antipathy quickly turns to sympathy.

Ambivalence can also mean inconsistency. He praises the train that allows the masses to visit the hills, yet is scornful of other technological advances when they offend his aesthetics. He feels the mountains should be open to all, nevertheless destroys a cache of petrol stowed by the riders of scramble bikes. He feels women would be better stewards of the environment but, if he had his wish, might not a battalion of Margaret Thatchers catapult themselves out of the woodwork?

Of course, these are not the bald contradictions that my assertions might make them appear. There are sound and reasoned arguments against destroying peaceful valleys for profit-making purposes, macho male posturing and the unnecessary use of machinery which destroys the ecology. Yet, the suggested dichotomy does seem to be at the heart of the problem. If you damage the environment, no matter how minimally, with your own recreational activities, there is always the danger that someone may cast the first stone in the direction of your particular glass house.

In that respect Perrin's writings, at times, lack the political steadfastness of an Orwell or even a Doughty. I am then reminded of the former's essay on Charles Dickens. Not so much the gibe of 'rotten architecture but wonderful gargoyles' (though there is an occasional tendency in that direction) but rather the problem caused by Dickens' unswerving support of the underdog. So, though he loathes the

Catholic Church and even more the Aristocracy, Dickens has to support both in *Barnaby Rudge* and *A Tale of Two Cities* when it is their turn to be put under the cosh. This leaves the reader uncertain as to what the author's views really are or, worse, how seriously he believes in the causes he chooses to espouse.

But *Yes, to Dance* is by no means all moral maze and much of the old delight of simply being among the hills and in the company of friends remains. Nowhere more so than in 'On a Summer's Night', first published in *Climber and Hillwalker* in 1989, which I feel contains all that is best in Perrin's writing. The outline of the article is straightforward. On impulse one evening, as much for company as climbing, Perrin persuades a friend, Judy Yates, to join him in an expedition to Carreg Alltrem. After a variety of delays they reach the crag and climb Lavaredo Wall, finishing up in the pub to celebrate a satisfactory event.

The bare facts are little more than pegs on which to hang other tales and, as always when Perrin is at his best, the delight, rather than the devil, is in the detail. He starts by taking the reader into his confidence: 'Think of the best times you've had climbing … It's a fair bet …' and he's got you with him. Even if you have never climbed Lavaredo Wall or even been to Carreg Alltrem on a summer's evening, you are one of the party. In fact, in such good humour that you can also put up with the delays caused by the mystery tours run by every coach operator in North Wales. These arrive in the Lledr Valley not only at the same time as those opposedly bound for the fleshpots of Llandudno, but also at the precise point in the road where coaches can pass 'so long as each driver is prepared to think millimetres and not no-claims bonuses'. Even the imprecation of a jobsworth, whose 'usual amalgam of references to copulation, departure, illegitimacy and Forestry Commission Regulations' prevents your driving to the foot of the crag, can be a source of amusement rather than annoyance.

In fact, the walk is a bonus in which you can examine the remains of a ruined farmhouse, recall the trout supper caught years ago, flee, to avoid the midges, those 'swirling spirals of venomous, shrieking infinitesimals', into the sun and the breeze that blows 'like the settling of clean cool sheets'. All this amid the talk of other climbs and other days. The route itself is a delight where verticality is compensated by good holds. The top pitch 'looks as if it could be any grade from VS to E6' but nervousness turns to revelation as 'wherever your hands wander they sink two-finger-joints-deep into the sharpest holds imaginable'. Contented elation that later joins forces with the woman in the Bryn Tyrch who, after a successful day at Tremadog, is determined on Cloggy for the morrow.

'Yes, to dance beneath the diamond sky/With one hand waving free...' Only Perrin can know what exact images were in his mind when he chose the title for his second collection but I suspect that those captured 'On a Summer's Night' come close.

More Things in Heaven and Earth

 In 1950 Wilfred Noyce published a collection of essays entitled *Scholar Mountaineers*. He examines in turn a number of key figures who, he argues, have contributed to the modern movement of mountaineering. They range from Dante to Leslie Stephen, visiting *en route* Petrarch, Rousseau, Goethe, the Wordsworths, Keats and Ruskin. In his introduction, he explains what binds them together:

Men of all ages have looked at mountains and have interpreted them in the light of their own social and religious needs. For each age they have filled a gap to complete its picture, even when the finishing touch needed was no more than a distant backcloth. Thus they have provided buttresses for theism, consolations to the atheists, weighty arguments to the cynic or satisfying examples to the pantheist. Philosophers have looked and have meditated, then they have pronounced upon them. But behind their pronouncements the mountains stand still smiling

and inscrutable. We will mean for you what you wish, they seem to say. What we really are, you can never know.

If Noyce is right, it would take a brave individual who, having decided what mountains and mountaineering are all about, should go to press with his particular pronouncement and risk the ridicule of some latter-day Hamlet. However, in 1952 Oliver & Boyd published a book by R B Frere, entitled *Thoughts of a Mountaineer*, which seemed willing to do just that. The author traces his climbing experiences, which occurred during and immediately after the Second World War, and places them in their historical context. Much of his reaction is emotionally charged and his sentimental fervour can make for uncomfortable reading for those nurtured on *fin de siècle* cynicism. There is a lack of that ironic deprecation we have come to expect from those who plodge into the quagmire of 'What is Life all about?' In Frere's case, friends seem too good to be true, always cheerful under adversity, uncomplaining whatever the circumstance, and his world of mountaineers appears to be populated with paragons of virtue and worth.

Moreover, an uncritical respect for his elders permeates the work. On one occasion a 'mature mountaineer' takes the author on his first 'proper climb' and promptly bottles the crux. Rather than retreat, he hands over the lead to the novice, justifying the decision on the grounds that he, the heavier man, is better equipped to arrest a fall. Rather than comment on his companion's pusillanimity, or even offer some reappraisal of the true nature of maturity, Frere waxes enthusiastic as he recalls the 'tremendous elation' that filled him on being deemed fit to lead a pitch that had defeated the expert.

Although it is not wise to judge a book by its cover, first impressions count and in this case the chosen image is one of the three wise mountaineers, deep in thought as they plod up a not particularly steep slope, silhouetted against the darkening sky. When the photograph appears in the text, the symbolism is glossed with the caption 'We walked in almost unbroken silence.' Perhaps the writer hopes that the insertion of 'almost' will hint at matters of untold significance. This use of modifiers more for effect than clarification tends to have a rather different effect on the reader.

Nor do the climbs described within suggest the pushing back of boundaries either mental or physical. Frere considered that three years of experience was necessary before it was advisable to visit Skye and then only in the company of an experienced companion. The descriptions of straightforward routes are overwritten and an ascent of Suilven by what appears the easiest route attains the proportions of a minor epic. On top of this, the literary trappings do not suggest an incisive investigation. 'The First Soft Notes', 'Halcyon Days' and 'Ghosts of the Past' as chapter titles are more Barbara Cartland than Walter Bonatti. Yet, despite these misgivings, closer inspection shows that there is a sincere and thoughtful attempt to discover why we climb or, at least, to engage profoundly with that question.

The book opens with a prologue in which Frere and two friends chance upon a long-abandoned farmhouse in Mid Lairgs. They try the door but it is locked. About to leave, they hear a loud click and see that their efforts have caused the rusted padlock to snap and fall from its fastening. They enter and find among the debris a small pram, sufficiently decayed to suggest that its most recent occupant must be by now fully grown. A second visit confirms that they can use the Farm as a base for the odd weekend when they have no plans for bigger hills. With the owner's permisssion (no Creagh Dhu appropriation here) they do it up and decide to celebrate the arrival of 1941 on the summit of nearby Beinn a Bheurlaich. Stirred by the night's events and too much strong tea, Frere, unable to sleep, is possessed by memories and passes the hours trying to recall what it was that first drew him to the hills. His account that follows is a distillation of these memories and closes, again at the Farm, with a summative epilogue.

Prologue and epilogue each act as a flying buttress to hold together the main body of the book. This is carefully structured and divided into three sections: 'Early Morning', 'Late Morning' and 'High Noon'. There is a consequent sense of progression, as with the occupant of the pram, from early experience and awareness, through the achievements built on a growing sense of confidence to a traumatic account of self doubt and internal turmoil when tragedy ultimately occurs. Although superficially a description of days on the hills, it is, as the flyleaf suggests, a journey from youth to manhood. As with most of the genre, the various milestones are marked with their own epiphany and gather around them appropriate symbolic images. In addition, each part has its own parallel structure that traces, like a rock climb of varied and various pitches, a path from tentative beginnings, through failure and success, to a point that plateaus on temporary closure.

The first section, 'Early Morning', is a literary exploration of early memories and experiences. The author tries a variety of approaches to produce a valid re-creation. He recalls his first day in the hills as a child and attempts to analyse his remembered feelings. Although the detail remains clear, he finds the result of his analysis unsatisfactory. He realises that later experience dissects and rearranges earlier events and feelings for its own purposes, that the act of recapturing can be an act of 'murder'. The child might have had a truer understanding, but whatever he had has by now been warped by time and the resurrected images could, Frere fears, be a perversion of that truth.

The second chapter changes tack. Rather than dissect and explain, he allows the images to work for themselves, to create sensation rather than exposition. He details his first proper climb and the account is pervaded by a series of tight contrasts. Throughout the day an eagle freely soars and dives, as the two climbers, one old, one young, laboriously work their way up the rock face. The cliff itself is a contradiction. From below it looks a continuous sheet of granite but from above, because it is seamed with sloping heathery ledges, it appears nothing more than a steep but straightforward hillside. Other perceptions also confuse. The light he looked at was afternoon light on the hillside but evening light in the valley. Through it all, the eagle continues to soar and dive. It is as though Frere hopes the conjunction of these contradictory images might form a blade to cut into a consciousness dulled by the mundanity of normal life. A sharp-edged instrument that might expose his feelings for the hills. As he explains, 'There is a limit to what I say I have seen: but none to what I have felt.'

The third chapter, 'The Dwelling Place of Beauty', is more overtly symbolic. The writer crosses a bridge perilously poised above a gorge of continuous cas-cading water. This and the bones of a rabbit mould-ering into the earth make him accept himself and his surroundings as but one moment in a cycle, rather than any individual and separate entity. He was at once 'shaggy caveman ... primitive herdsman ... cau-tious clansman'. Here around him, he feels, is the Truth. A path leads out of the ravine into a valley. As evening falls, he comes across a deserted building. Water drips, straw rustles, a door bangs to. Ecstasy gives way to dread but light begins to pervade the room as it is bathed in moonlight. In an epiphanal moment, realising that his understanding is limited by his ego, he undertakes a rapturous ascent of a nearby hillside. Slowly the 'drug' wears off and there is a toilsome return into the 'mutable world to which [he] was bound by the chains of custom'.

The writing is probably too overwrought for the chapter to be completely successful but there is a power and energy in the ideas that feed the language, which in turn sustains and reaffirms the ideas. Moreover, there is one moment when he develops an interesting technique to assist recall. He closes his eyes for several minutes before opening them like a camera shutter to imprint the scene on his mind. In the final chapter of the first section he employs the method to 'photograph' the vista from the summit of Sgurr nan Gillean on his first visit to Skye. This visit to the 'Valhalla of Rocks' is a fitting closure to the first section, which deals with the author's apprenticeship. The chapter title seems rather clichéd but perhaps there is more to it than immediately meets the eye. The Nordic connection is not inappropriate when discussing the western seaboard of Scotland and, although there is no etymological connection, 'val' is a common enough suffix attached to the hills in this region. More significantly, at the time of writing, Skye was indeed the end of the road for the average British mountaineer. Currency restrictions and set holiday patterns limited foreign travel and, for the majority, the Alps were no more than a dream. The Cuillin with its unique rock architecture and big hill feel was a reasonable culmination for those who wished to feed with the Gods.

The second section, 'Late Morning', seems to take the concept of man merging with Nature rather too literally. A visit to Suilven opens with the author being rescued from the miasmic hinterland into which he had sunk, and the combination of crag, bog and pond adds up to 'a strange place, devoid of the familiar props which hold the mind in balance.' In fact, when it comes to mountains, Frere seems attracted to the unusual or, at least, out of the way. The central chapter in the section is an account of the first ascent of Savage Slit, led by the author in 1945. The climb is on No 4 Buttress of Coire an Lochain on Cairngorm and its major feature is a 200-foot crack that splits the rock and disappears for several yards into the buttress. Progress is made by chimneying up the mountain's innards until a traverse can be made out of the depths on to the exposed outer edge of the fissure. The fact that such a striking line at a straightforward standard had not been previously attempted shows the potential extent of Scottish mountaineering and underlines the remoteness of the area in the days before private transport became the norm. More importantly, Frere seems to connect this remoteness of place and the intricacies involved in solving the problem with his own exploration of the outer reaches of his environment and so, by extension, the more remote and intricate parts of himself.

Nor was this the only burrowing. In the summative chapter of the section, back on Skye, his holiday ambition is first to 'force a passage through the cavernous Bhasteir gorge' through a combination of swimming and climbing, then complete an ascent of the Bhasteir Tooth by a subterranean chimney originally climbed in 1906 by Shadbolt and Maclaren. This tortuous route involves climbing the recess until a tunnel can be reached which, after twenty feet, doubles back on itself to allow an exit, as through a trapdoor, on to the tip of the Tooth itself. There is no clear explanation as to where the attraction lay in these ventures. No doubt a psychologist could make something of a desire to reprise the experience of being bent double in a dark and damp cavity. Indeed, Frere likens his arrival at the top of the Tooth to a baby being born. A cynic, however, might feel that a desire for a return to the security of the womb was more real than metaphorical.

The final section, 'High Noon,' has a sombre tone and reflects the inner turmoil and tension of the film that bears that title. There are also echoes of Wordsworth's 'The Prelude', where early innocence is replaced by troubled pleasure. The first two chapters deal with the consequence of failure, failure that is heightened when contrasted with previous or subsequent success. Not for the first time, ecstasy and despair are seen as two sides of the same coin, rather than diametrically opposed emotions. Two days of undertaking climbs of 'the greatest severity' are followed by retreat from a straightforward snow and ice climb on the Ben and, on another occasion, within twenty-four hours of the author's timidity spoiling the day for the rest of the party he is involved in a new route on Rannoch Wall.

It seems at this point that the implications of the greater struggle being enacted across Europe make a firmer connection with climbing in Frere's mind.

On the new route just mentioned, there is an alarming incident. He has moved to an inadequate ledge to give his leader the maximum of moral support. Leaning forward at one point to see how things were progressing, he is horrified to discover his apparently substantial belay moving forward with him. It is clear that if his companion were to fall there would be nothing he could do to prevent them both finishing in a heap on the screes several hundred feet below. Of course, he has to suffer in silence until the pitch is completed and he can safely despatch the offending block to its, rather than their, final resting place.

Between the cognisance and the outcome there was considerable opportunity for conjecture and what most struck him was that, at the very moment they were 'jeopardising [themselves] for the satisfaction of a mad whim', others were 'giving their lives for the country'. Virtually all the events in his account had taken place against the backdrop of the Second World War, but previously hostilities had only intruded in that they limited climbing opportunities to snatches of leave or their demands denied individuals a part in the various adventures. Now, waiting in the mist for a sign of the slip that would end all speculation, the arbitrary nature of it all plants a seed that will grow, as the section proceeds, into a question of black despair. Why should this man die and that man live?

The general becomes the particular when he learns soon afterwards that John, his companion on the Rannoch Wall climb, has been killed, along with his second, while attempting a new route in Sgoran Dubh. It was a climb he and John had planned to try together when circumstance permitted. The guilt often associated with fortuitous survival takes over and the author enters into 'a period of profound misery'. The product of this state is a chapter entitled 'Alone in Solitude' that in its language and imagery of destruction and nihilism acts as a negative foil to 'The Dwelling Place of Beauty', the uplifting third piece of the first section. The misery lasted two long years and was only resolved by another moment of chance. Foul weather and poor navigation had benighted Frere and friend in Glen Einich. They sought shelter in first the Upper Bothy, then the Lower Bothy, only to find that each had been pulled down by either man or nature.

The symbolic implication of destruction and decay, coupled with the fact that they were now forced to stop in the shadow of Sgoran Dubh, the hill that had killed his friend, was not lost on him. However, his companion persuades him to help rebuild a rough shelter out of the debris, which, in turn, enables Frere to fall into a fitful sleep where his feverish mind is overtaken by violent and troubling images. The effect is cathartic and on waking he climbs to the summit to make peace with himself and the hill.

The epilogue returns to the Farm and seems to be an extension of the prologue. Frere awakes to 'the anticlimactic knowledge of cold feet and a dying fire', his companions still asleep, exhausted by the night's exertions. It is as though all we have read between start and finish is as in a dream. As with all dreams, time does not necessarily follow its normally accepted sequence. Historically, the ascent of Savage Slit occurred five years after the new Girdle Traverse of Rannoch Wall. So the death of John must have happened before at least some of the events that seem to be born of happier times.

In fact, it appears that 'John' is not John at all. The SMC guide credits the first ascent of the Girdle Traverse to H I Ogilvy and R Frere in June 1940. Similarly, the 'Kenneth' who was Frere's second on Savage Slit is, according to the Cairngorm guide,

J D Walker. It is therefore reasonable to assume that his companions 'Jimmy' and 'Norman' aren't as stated either, and that the 'Jimmy' of one chapter might not necessarily be the 'Jimmy' of another. In fact, the use of Christian names is quite unusual in itself. The normal practice at the time was surnames (Bill Murray referred even to his brother-in-law as MacAlpine) or, if there was an attempt at stiff-lipped intimacy, a full set of initials.

By extension, it is possible to assume that the described episodes are not exact reproductions of actual events, or even that the events actually occurred. It is only at this point that you realise that this collection of memories is less a man turning over stones on the beach of his past experience than an attempt to create a work as a whole in the manner of a novel or collection of connected short stories. Frere may be blending character and events to produce not an absolute record but a self-contained piece of literature. Perhaps, after all, *Thoughts of a Mountaineer* is not a climbing book at all, any more than *Ulysses* is a Dublin A-Z.

Thirty-five years later another book on climbing appeared which also seemed to harbour a greater ambition than that of a mere record or gazetteer.

Native Stones by David Craig is, according to the blurb, a book that 'engages profoundly with the human dimension of mountaineering'. Nevertheless, it had an interesting baptism by way of critical review. Jim Perrin, who contributed the above sentiment, adding for good measure that, with the book's 'breadth of context and precision of language, it would deserve to rank as a classic in the literature of any sport', later appeared to perform a rather spectacular somersault when asked to review it for *The Independent*.*

In fact, I probably bought the book in the first place because of Perrin's endorsement. At the time, I only glanced through it, noting that as the emphasis was on climbing in this country, it could be a useful addition to my literary researches into British mountaineering. If the last term is to mean more than rambling around the hills and to imply a degree of danger and technical skill, then rock climbing at a high standard is an important part of these islands' portfolio. The selection of routes that

---

*I have recently discovered that the remarks on the book's jacket were no more than a puff based on a rather cursory reading of the proofs. It was only when asked by *The Independent* to review the book that Perrin formed a considered opinion.

sprang from the page suggested that, if there were any profound engagement by the author in the relationship between man and these particular stones, it could well be of significant interest.

When I then came across Perrin's review with its apparent change of heart, I felt that the time had come when I ought to read the book properly and make up my own mind. Perrin's later criticism has two main strands. First, that the language, far from having the 'precision' he seemingly first praised, is on closer inspection dislocated and at times self-indulgent; second, that most damning of faint praise, he felt there was probably quite a decent book hidden amongst the undergrowth.

My initial reaction was that either the critic's and my view of self-indulgent writing did not coincide, or that, in an attempt to redress the balance, Perrin had allowed the pendulum to swing too far the other way. The epigraph and opening paragraph of *Native Stones* certainly grab the attention. There is a different technique at work from the climbing writing norm. Craig is a poet and as such is understandably interested in the relationship that exists between the written word and the emotions, and also whether the compression that imagery allows can be a better medium for exposition than discursive prose. Chapter 2 is a poem of twenty-one lines which reworks the ideas that take place in the first five prose pages of Chapter 1. The distillation works well. Perrin's observation of a 'precision of language' that encompasses a 'breadth of context' is clearly apparent.

Nor is this an isolated occurrence. At various points in the book, the procedure is repeated. After a detailed account of stripping a crag of its vegetation in order to achieve the ego-satisfying completion of a new route, there is a poem entitled 'Against Looting' that starts 'Leave the mahogany where it is!' And following the death of Bill Peascod, who accompanied the author on many of the Lake District climbs described, there is a poem, 'The Veterans', that praises just such famous men. The problem is when the 'poetry' trips up the prose. Perrin is understandably irritated by such figurative expressions that describe the surface of stones as though they were 'the stomachs of very old Mediterranean tramps', or climbers as 'parasites in the pelt of a bear', and it is easy to see why. The difficulty with similes is that they specifically invite the reader to visualise the comparison. If the comparison appears absurd or the reader has to strain to make the connection, the point of the exercise is lost. In the same way, the summoning of T S Eliot or Ezra Pound to lend quasi-philosophical weight to an argument of the moment can be more confusing than helpful, particularly if the reader's understanding of the quoted passage is at odds with that of the author.

The outcome is that the book, unlike Frere's, appears to have no internal discipline that holds it together, no conscious attempt to develop a pattern or argument out of the accumulation of experience. It is a journey through remembered events recounted in roughly chronological order. Associated with each event is usually a larger, more discursive point. Craig could well argue that is exactly what he intended—a series of essays and assorted pieces of poetry which the reader can dip into and out of at will. But people, when presented with a volume, tend to read it as a whole and expect some sort of editorial consistency. There are times when opinions delivered at one point are apparently contradicted at another, and there are times when the map goes missing altogether.

Take the passage that deals with a medley of sheep rescues. Although it is an account of three separate occasions, you tend, and are probably intended, to read it as a piece. Craig argues that it is reasonable for climbers to rescue cragfast sheep. Sheep have been bred by man in such a way that they have lost their natural agility. Moreover man, in order to maximise his resources, has provided such poor pasture that the beasts are forced to risk life and limb to find anything worth eating. So man should try to redress the balance. A valid point and worth exploring. But the force of the argument is deflected by a series of asides that take a disproportionate part in the debate. The idea, for example, that sheep are unable to escape because they have been denied access to guidebooks is an amusing enough piece of whimsy but seems rather out of place.

What is more, these digressions seem to confuse Craig's original point that the reason behind salvaging cragfast sheep is a moral one. Man put it there, so man (in the absence of ovine literacy classes) should leap to the rescue. In fact, the deflection appears to have changed the direction of the argument significantly. It is now not so much a moral imperative as a commercial one, a repayment of a debt to the farmers who facilitate the author's recreational activities by creating paths. That is, the farmer who effectively put the sheep there in the first place. The passage now seems to have lost whatever way it had and dissolves into Man as Hero (comparisons of taking on an All Black Pack single-handed) and Man as Saint/Protector (image of sheep draped round shepherd's shoulders) who, when the good deeds are done, collectively pat themselves on the back over a pint at the local hostelry.

So there are times when I agree with Perrin that you can become distracted by the detail but I would argue that a very good book, or even books, lurks or lurk within the volume and the reader could profit by putting aside any personal objections to discover that potential. First, there is the author's real sense of place, particularly within the climbing context. Everyone who has had the experience knows that there is a world of difference between climbing on a sea cliff and on a similar piece of rock marooned in the middle of a moor, but it is not as easy to put the difference into words. Chapter 17 is a fine evocation of being on 'the very fulcrum between ... the above and the below'. This develops into an exploration of the relationship between his ideas of balancing between the sea and the sky and the structure of Bill Peascod's elemental paintings that illuminates both art and climbing. A more sustained examination of how and why we attempt to capture transience in a permanent form would be welcome.

Chapter 19 poses another interesting point. Do we climb mountains to be part of them, warming our hands on them as it were, or as an opportunity to excite the emotions and thereby inflate the ego? Craig calls various mountain philosophers as witness. Among the usual suspects, Wordsworth and Coleridge are there to represent the poles of his argument. Much more could have been made of this. There is not the depth that is explored in *Scholar Mountaineers*, but Noyce stops at Leslie Stephen. Craig extends the argument into the twentieth century, through Murray and Edwards to Alvarez and Drummond. On this occasion, at least, less does not necessarily mean more.

But the most unusual and, in some ways, unique nature of the book is the result of Craig coming to the cliff face in middle age. As a result, he spends much of his early climbing days under the tutelage of his offspring, who had been taught to climb as part of their formal education. This inversion allows an interesting take on the child being father of the man and the resulting freedom he encourages in his children contrasts neatly with his own repressed formative experience. When supported by autobiographical detail such as this, the book (as Perrin admits) rattles on apace and for those of a certain age it must rekindle the remembered panic, the recalled pleasure, that accompanies parenthood. Eventually even the youngest child has outstripped the climbing skills of his progenitor and as Neil, last in the line, puts it, when Craig yet again fails to climb Kipling Groove without the support of a filial rope, 'Tough luck, Dad—you've run out of sons.'

But there is the other side of the coin which Craig can explore. Unlike Frere, who felt his initial reactions to climbing had been distorted by time, Craig is investigating his novitiate without such interference. Moreover, he can bring a mature understanding of language and history to bear, to try to explain to himself what he is doing and why he is doing it. As he put it, 'I climb with my feet on solid rock and my head in a dense cloud of thoughts.' He can measure his anxieties as to whether a pitch will go against the Yeats poem 'An Irish Airman Foresees His Death' and place the framework of his own lifetime over the history of the routes he is now climbing.

The latter preoccupation prevails through the text. He must have realised that if, like his children, he had started climbing in his teens and at that time been able to climb the routes he was now completing, he would have been at the cutting edge of the new wave that sprang into life in the late forties and early fifties. He must have thought, if I could rewind the time…

Much of the book is, consciously or sub-consciously, concerned with this possibility. The routes described read like a wish list for climbers of the fifties. Two, Kipling Groove and Birkett's Harlot Face on the Castle Rock of Triermain, loom large in the text and, in the case of the latter, obsessively in his mind. As part of the time machine, he seeks out the climbing company of the pioneers of that period, Birkett, Peascod and Greenwood. He even persuades the last named to come out of retirement. To complete the fantasy, he at times climbs with Peascod with no more gear than a hemp rope and a couple of slings. Perrin describes all this as bizarre and perhaps it is. But it is also interesting.

At least it gives one insight into why men climb— a desire to be part of a particular historical jigsaw. But there have to be more compelling reasons than that if broken necks are in the offing. As Hamlet implies, all questions of 'how' and 'why' are sufficiently complicated to throw up their own smokescreen and those that pertain to climbing are no exception. Mallory's response, probably not by chance, is careful to avoid a precise definition of whatever 'it' really is. The books by Frere and Craig may have their imperfections and, like Horatio, their vision might be limited but, in trying to work out what makes them climb at all, they make a significant contribution to the debate.

Malachi

The implication of my opening remarks was that, by the early seventies, an end had been reached in climbing in Britain. And it is tempting to suggest that the particular nature of the writings I have drawn upon has, by now, similarly run its course. The recent appearance of Jim Perrin's *The Climbing Essays*, a retrospective collection that ranges over a lifetime, suggests that he, at least, has drawn some sort of line. So, if the prophets and judges have had their say and suitable lamentations have been made, it is interesting to speculate what any new testament might herald.

Like climbing itself, there will always remain odd corners and cracks to fill. There will also, after a decent interval, be a reappraisal of leading individuals and their achievements, but the back does seem to have been well and truly broken. History has shown, however, that no sooner does such a proclamation appear, than it is swept away by a new wave of exploration. Nevertheless, there are compelling reasons why some of the old formats will not resurface. Paternalism, as the accepted norm, has gone; so, too, the lofty pronouncements and stern warnings that often formed the backbone of instructional manuals. In any event, with the rise of outdoor activities as part of the educational process, instruction these days tends to be practical rather than theoretical.

Even guidebooks have changed. Once they were lined with praise for famous men and embroidered with every twist and turn that ingenuity could invent. Now they are often reduced to the bare bones, where the photographic topo rather than the written word holds sway. What once was Mrs Beeton is now more Delia Smith. It will only be a matter of time before a website appears featuring every climb in the country, to which surfers may add their own contribution in, no doubt, their own inimitable style. Moreover, Clubland is not what it was and the time allowed for a slower-moving age to produce thoughtful pieces for the journals they espoused has been steadily eroded.

But it is more than a question of social mores. Arguably, the best example of writing that captures the essence of British climbing is Dorothy Pilley's *Climbing Days*. Its attraction was that it dealt with climbs and cliffs that were familiar to the general readership and, as it was the accepted practice to work up through the grades, the writing struck a chord with successive generations. How many in the twenty-first century set out for her much admired and desired Direct Route on Glyder Fach, or choose to catch an airborne leader rather than reel him in on a system of pulleys?

These two examples lie at the heart of the discussion. First, the Direct Route isn't. It contains various alternatives at a variety of grades. Like the New West on Pillar or Great Slab on Cloggy, it was a key that unlocks the cliff. The dramatic nature of such convoluted routes is that round every corner can lie an insuperable difficulty or a surprising challenge. When this drama is exploited in the written word by a Murray or Gervasutti, the reader too strains in anticipation of what is to come. But when climbs become increasingly featureless, there is as little for the reader to grasp as there is for today's E-men. It is hard, therefore, to envisage *Climbing Wall Days* or *Unknown Climbing Walls* as winners of the Boardman Tasker Prize. Second, much of the romance has gone. When Pilley's husband decided it was better to abandon a probably inadequate belay and manually field the leader who was plunging headfirst towards him and mutual oblivion, there was an obvious human dimension to engage the emotions. Today our hero sets off carrying enough blocks and tackle to start a small shipyard and it seems only a matter of time before the faithful second becomes equally robotic.

So, unless the shades of 'Whipplesnaith' stalk the land and wall climbing goes al fresco on the great monuments that populate our cities, fiction seems the way forward. Perhaps M John Harrison's *Climbers* will be seminal in this respect. It is not about climbers or climbing in the presumed sense of the word, nor is the word used ironically or as some sort of pun. Rock climbing on distinctly non-Arcadian outcrops provides merely a framework for a novel about life in Thatcherite Britain. But it could only be written by an author who understands the sport, as the characters move about, restlessly searching for 'the perfect climb'. As earlier writers used their leisured erudition to provide in their writings the poise and balance they had discovered in their new pastime, so might the intensity of modern-day climbing provide the messenger 'who shall sit as a refiner and purifer of silver' mined by a former age.

Bibliography

The books listed below are concerned with the story of mountaineering in Britain. Some are exclusively so, others do not confine their attention to these shores alone. But between them they give a pretty fair picture of the people and places that have contributed to the development of British climbing in its first hundred years. There are also some examples of fiction (asterisked) which have British mountaineering at the centre rather than the edge. As with all lists, there are no doubt omissions but if you get through all these you will have made a fairly decent start.

Abraham, A P: *Rock-climbing in Skye* (Longmans 1908)

Abraham, G D: *British Mountain Climbs* (Mills & Boon 1909); *The Complete Mountaineer* (Methuen 1907); *Modern Mountaineering* (Methuen 1933); *Rock-climbing in North Wales* (G P Abraham 1906)

Allan, E: *Burn on the Hill* (Bidean Books 1995)

Alvarez, A: *Feeding the Rat* (Bloomsbury 1988)

Bagley, A L: *Holiday Rambles in the English Lake District* (Skeffington 1925); *Holiday Rambles in North Wales* (Skeffington 1920); *Walks and Scrambles in the Highlands* (Skeffington 1914)

Baker, E A: *The British Highlands with Rope and Rucksack* (Witherby 1933); *The Highlands with Rope and Rucksack*

(Witherby 1923); *Moors, Crags and Caves of the High Peak and the Neighbourhood* (Heywood 1903); *On Foot in the Highlands* (Maclehose 1932)

Banks, M E B: *Commando Climber* (Dent 1955)

Barford, J E Q: *Climbing in Britain* (Penguin Books 1946)

Barrow, J: *Mountain Ascents in Westmoreland and Cumberland* (Sampson Low 1886)

Bell, J H B, Bozman, E F & Blakeborough, J F: *British Hills and Mountains* (Batsford 1940); *A Progress in Mountaineering* (Oliver & Boyd 1950)

Bennet, D: *Scottish Mountain Climbs* (Batsford 1979)

Benson, C E: *British Mountaineering* (Routledge 1909); *Crag and Hound in Lakeland* (Hurst & Blackett 1902)

Bingley, W: *A Tour round North Wales, Performed during the Summer of 1798* (Williams 1800)

Birkett, B: *Classic Rock Climbs in Great Britain* (Oxford Illustrated Press 1988); *Classic Rock Climbs in Northern England* (Oxford Illustrated Press 1990); *Classic Rock Climbs in Southern England* (Oxford Illustrated Press 1991); *Lakeland's Greatest Pioneers* (Hale 1983)

Borthwick, A: *Always a Little Further* (Faber 1939; reprinted Diadem Books 1993)

Bowker, T: *Mountain Lakeland* (Hale 1984)

Brown, D & Mitchell, I: *Mountain Days and Bothy Nights* (Luath Press 1987); *A View from the Ridge* (The Ernest Press 1991)

Brown, H M: *Climbing the Corbetts* (Gollancz 1988); *Hamish's Groats End Walk* (Gollancz 1981); *Hamish's Mountain Walk* (Gollancz 1978)

Brown, J: *The Hard Years* (Gollancz 1967)

Butterfield, I: *The High Mountains of Britain and Ireland* (Diadem Books 1985)

Byne, E & Sutton, G: *High Peak: the Story of Walking & Climbing in the Peak District* (Secker & Warburg 1966)

Caldwell, C: *Climb Every Mountain* (Macdonald & Co 1990)

*Carr, G: *Death on Milestone Buttress* (Bles 1951); *Fat Man's Agony* (Bles 1969); *Swing Away Climber* (Bles 1959)

Carr, H R C & Lister, G A: *The Mountains of Snowdonia* (Bodley Head 1925)

Clark, R W & Pyatt, E C: *Mountaineering in Britain* (Phoenix 1957)

Cleare, J S & Collomb, R G: *Sea Cliff Climbing in Britain* (Constable 1973)

Cooper, W H: *The Hills of Lakeland* (Warne 1938)

Connor, J: *Creagh Dhu Climber* (The Ernest Press 1999)

*Coxhead, E: *One Green Bottle* (Faber 1951)

Craig, D: *Native Stones* (Secker & Warburg 1987)

Dean, S: *Hands of a Climber* (The Ernest Press 1993)

Docharty, W McK: *A Selection of Some 900 British and Irish Mountain Tops* (Darien Press 1954); Supplement to above Volume I (Darien Press 1962); Supplement to above Volume II (Darien Press 1962)

Doughty, J H: *Hill-writings of J H Doughty* (Rucksack Club 1937)

Drasdo, H: *The Ordinary Route* (The Ernest Press 1997)

Drummond, G J F: *A Dream of White Horses* (Diadem Books 1987)

*Dutton, G J F: *The Ridiculous Mountains* (Diadem Books 1984); *The Complete Doctor Stories: The Ridiculous Mountains* and *Nothing So Simple As Climbing* (Bâton Wicks 1997)

Frere, R B: *Thoughts of a Mountaineer* (Oliver & Boyd 1952)

Gray, D D: *Rope Boy* (Gollancz 1970)

Griffin, A. H: *Adventuring in Lakeland* (Hale 1980); *In Mountain*

Lakeland (Guardian Press 1963); *In the Real Lakeland* (Guardian Press 1961); *Long Days in the Hills* (Hale 1974)

Hall, R W: *The Art of Mountain Tramping* (Witherby 1932); *On Cumbrian Fells* (Whitehaven News 1926)

Hankinson, A: *Camera on the Crags* (Heinemann 1975); *The First Tigers* (Dent 1972); *The Mountain Men* (Heinemann 1977)

Harker, G: *Easter Climbs* (Sherratt & Hughes 1913)

*Harrison, M J: *Climbers* (Gollancz 1989)

'Hederatus': *Cambridge Nightclimbing* (Chatto & Windus 1970)

Hewitt, D: *Walking the Watershed* (Tacit Press 1994)

*Hubank, R: *Hazard's Way* (The Ernest Press 2001)

Humble, B H: *The Cuillin of Skye* (Hale 1952); *On Scottish Hills* (Chapman & Hall 1948); *Tramping in Skye* (Grant & Murray 1933)

Jones, O G: *Rock-climbing in the English Lake District* (Longman 1897; facsimile reprint of 2nd edn E J Morten 1973)

Kirkus, C F: *Let's Go Climbing* (Nelson 1941; reprinted Ripping Yarns 2004)

*Lefebure, M: *Scratch & Co: the Great Cat Expedition* (Gollancz 1968)

McNeish, C & Else, R: *The Edge: 100 years of Scottish Mountaineering* (BBC Books 1994)

Milburn, G (ed), Walker, D & Wilson, K: *The First Fifty Years* (BMC 1997)

Milner, C D: *Rock for Climbing* (Chapman & Hall 1950)

Moffat, G: *Space Below My Feet* (Hodder & Stoughton 1961)

Monkhouse, F & Williams, J: *Climber and Fellwalker in Lakeland* (David & Charles 1972)

*Montague, C E: *Fiery Particles* (Chatto & Windus 1923)

Moran, M: *The Munros in Winter* (David & Charles 1986)

Murray, W H: *The Evidence of Things Not Seen* (Bâton Wicks 2002); *Mountaineering in Scotland* (Dent 1947); *Undiscovered Scotland* (Dent 1951)

Neate, W R: *Mountaineering and its Literature* (Cicerone Press 1978, revised edition 1986)

Nunn, P: *At the Sharp End* (Unwin Hyman 1988)

Oppenheimer, L J: *The Heart of Lakeland* (Sherratt & Hughes 1908)

Palmer, W T: *The Complete Hillwalker, Rock-climber and Cave Explorer* (Pitman 1934)

Patey, T W: *One Man's Mountains* (Gollancz 1971)

Peascod, W: *Journey after Dawn* (Cicerone Press 1985)

Perrin, J: *The Climbing Essays* (The In Pinn 2006); *Menlove: the Life of John Menlove Edwards* (Gollancz 1985); *On and Off the Rocks* (Gollancz 1986); *Yes, to Dance* (Oxford Illustrated Press 1990); *The Villain* (Hutchinson 2005)

Pilley, D: *Climbing Days* (Bell 1935)

Pyatt, E C: *A Climber in the West Country* (David & Charles 1968); *Climbing and Walking in South East England* (David & Charles 1970); *Where to Climb in the British Isles* (Faber 1960)

Pyatt, E C & Noyce, C W F: *British Crags and Climbers* (Dobson 1952)

Raeburn, H: *Mountaineering Art* (Fisher Unwin 1920)

*Rees, L & Harris, A: *Take it to the Limit* (Diadem Books 1981)

Richmond, W K: *Climber's Testament* (Redman 1950)

Robertson, D: *George Mallory* (Faber 1969)

Rudge, E C W: *Mountain Days Near Home* (W D Wharton 1941)

Russell, J: *Climb If You Will* (M J Russell 1974)

Salt, H S: *On Cambrian and Cumbrian Hills* (Fifield 1908)

Sandeman, R G: *A Mountaineer's Journal* (Druid Press 1948)

Sansom, G S: *Climbing at Wasdale before the First World War* (Castle Cary Press 1982)

Smith, W P H: *Climbing in the British Isles, Vol I: England* (Longmans 1894), *Volume II: Wales and Ireland*, with H C Hart (Longman 1895) (Facsimile reprint The Ernest Press 1986)

Smythe, A G: *Rock Climbers in Action in Snowdonia* (Secker & Warburg 1966)

*Somers, D: *Collected Short Stories* (Bâton Wicks 2004)

Soper, N J, Wilson, K & Crew, P: *The Black Cliff* (Kaye & Ward 1971)

Steven, C: *The Island Hills* (Hurst & Blackett 1955); *The Story of Scotland's Hills* (Hale 1975)

Styles, F S: *Mountains of North Wales* (Gollancz 1973); *Rock and Rope* (Faber 1967); *Shadow Buttress* (Faber 1959)

Sutton, G J S & Noyce, C W F: *Samson: the Life and Writings of Menlove Edwards* (Cloister Press 1961)

*Sutton, G: *Fell Days* (Museum Press 1948)

Thomson, I D S: *The Black Cloud* (The Ernest Press 1993); *May The Fire Be Always Lit* (The Ernest Press 1995)

Treacher, K: *Siegfried Herford: An Edwardian Rock-climber* (The Ernest Press 2000)

Turnbull, R: *The Riddle of Sphinx Rock: the Life and Times of Great Gable* (Millrace 2005)

Unsworth, W: *The English Outcrops* (Gollancz 1964); *This Climbing Game* (Viking 1984)

Walker, J H: *On Hills of the North* (Oliver & Boyd 1948)

Weir, T: *Highland Days* (Cassell 1948)

Westmorland, H: *Adventures in Climbing* (Pelham Books 1964)

Whillans, D D & Ormerod, A: *Don Whillans: Portrait of a Mountaineer* (Heinemann 1971)

'Whipplesnaith': *The Night Climbers of Cambridge* (Chatto & Windus 1937)

Wilson, G (ed): *The Central Buttress of Scafell* (Millrace 2004)

Wilson, K: *Classic Rock* (Granada 1978); *Cold Climbs* (Diadem Books 1983); *Hard Rock* (Hart Davis, MacGibbon 1974)

Wilson, K & Gilbert, R: *The Big Walks* (Diadem Books 1980); *Classic Walks* (Diadem Books 1982); *Wild Walks* (Diadem Books 1988)

Wright, J E B: *Rock-climbing in Britain* (Nicholas Kaye 1958); *Mountain Days in the Isle of Skye* (Moray Press 1934)

Young, G W: *Mountain Craft* (Methuen 1920); *Wall and Roof Climbing* (Spottiswood 1905)

Young, G W, Sutton, G J S & Noyce, C W F: *Snowdon Biography* (Dent 1957)

As has been suggested, the journals of various climbing clubs were often the springboard for mountain writing. The following is a list of the more readily available:

Cairngorm Club Journal (The Club 1893)

Climbers' Club Journal (The Club 1898)

Journal of the Fell and Rock Climbing Club of the English Lake District (The Club 1907)

Journal of the Karabiner Mountaineering Club (The Club 1950)

Ladies Scottish Climbing Club Journal (The Club 1929)

Pinnacle Club Journal (The Club 1924)

Rucksack Club Journal (The Club 1907)

Scottish Mountaineering Club Journal (SMC 1890)

Wayfarers' Club Journal (The Club 1928)

Yorkshire Ramblers' Club Journal (The Club 1899)